curious
kiwiwords

curious
kiwiwords

Max Cryer

HarperCollins*Publishers*

The author wishes to thank Henare te Ua, Joline de Lisa,
Richard Wolfe, Graeme Fisher, Robbie Ancell and Philip
O'Shea, New Zealand Herald of Arms Extraordinary.

National Library of New Zealand Cataloguing-in-Publication Data

Cryer, Max.
Curious Kiwi words / Max Cryer.
Includes bibliographical references.
ISBN: 1-86950-422-4
1. English language—Provincialisms—New Zealand.
2. English language—New Zealand—Semantics.
I. Title.
427.993—dc 21

First published 2002
HarperCollins*Publishers (New Zealand) Limited*
P.O. Box 1, Auckland

ISBN 1 86950 422 4

Set in Janson Text
Designed and typeset by Janine Brougham
Printed by Griffin Press, Australia on 79 gsm Bulky Paperback

Introduction

A New Zealand television programme once showed news footage of a group of English and American backpackers intending to enter an Auckland nightclub. Outside was a sign saying: 'Dress Code: NO *Swannies, Beanies, Singlets, Jandals or Gumboots*'.

The visitors were totally flummoxed: they didn't understand any of the words.

That was a special case. Nevertheless it is abundantly clear that, as a matter of course, New Zealanders use many words the meaning of which isn't always obvious to others. Or a word meaning something quite ordinary in New Zealand can mean something entirely different to people from another culture.

In no way are these oddities to be disparaged. This country has developed a dialect of its own as all communities do: it is possible to ride on a bus in Yorkshire, stand in a pub in Darwin or eat at a snack bar in Texas and not be able to understand any of the 'English-speaking' locals conversing around you. The same may be said of a stranger attending a rural stock sale in New Zealand.

The influences that formed New Zealand speech have been numerous. For several hundred years only one language was spoken here. Then in the 1800s came not just one other language but multiple dialect versions of that language: various regional kinds of English, plus Scottish, Welsh and Irish versions. Many of the words those early settlers brought to New Zealand have faded away completely in their mother country, but have remained in use here.

Later came settlers from China, the Netherlands, Poland, Dalmatia and Czechoslovakia, while soldiers, airmen and sailors went away to wars and then came home. And there has been fairly constant interaction with Australia, which also developed its own language style.

Cinema and television provided further major influences. New Zealand's purchasing power is small, but it is nonetheless able and, more significantly, willing, to purchase entertainment from two major vendors, Britain and the United States, besides offerings from Australia, and occasionally Canada. Thus, the average New Zealand home (and cinema) is exposed regularly to the vocabularies of *Coronation Street*, *ER* and *Blue Heelers* — three widely different language styles. Internationally, this is not common. Americans are not exposed to as much British television, or vice versa, as New Zealanders are to both.

Sometimes this situation results in what can only be called media osmosis, so that, with little resistance, people start saying taken out instead of bombed or bathroom when they mean toilet, simply because they've heard it on television!

But there also exists a stubborn resistance to change. Some stolidly New Zealand words and usages — bach, jandals, cheerios — remain, because that's what we say here.

Another slightly weird theory provides a possible contributing factor to New Zealand's particular speech style and vocabulary choice, namely false teeth. For many decades it was either a fashion or the norm for adult New Zealanders to have all their teeth out, even when there was no strong reason to do so. One result of this was a long-time caution about pronouncing anything that required too much muscular tension or mouth energy. A fairly narrow and unmoving oral style favoured words and phrases that could be spoken without the risk of dentures losing their anchor. Even when false teeth went out of fashion and people started to retain their own teeth, the upcoming generations had heard their parents' speech style and vocabulary and tended to perpetuate it.

In this collection, some words are unique to this country (obviously all the Maori words are), some are shared with Australia and quite a number are universal, but have a particular usage, flavour or popularity within New Zealand.

The text does not claim to be complete. Words and expressions slip into (and out of) the language almost every day. The *Oxford Dictionary of New Zealand English* took 45 years to compile and already some strange words have crept into New Zealand acceptance since it was published.

Like their forest namesake, Kiwis are constant foragers.

Q Afghan

A crunchy, chocolate-flavoured biscuit, usually containing cornflakes, covered with rich chocolate icing, and topped with a walnut. The biscuit and its name have been common in New Zealand since the 1930s and are believed to be so called simply because they are 'dark'!

Q Aggro

A slight confusion between the words aggravation (to make worse, to intensify) with aggression (over-readiness to attack) can be solved by using the term aggro, which came into use in the 1960s and could pass as an abbreviation of either. Technically, aggro is short for aggravation, which is often used to indicate annoyance and exasperation (though that is not its strict original sense, since it comes from the Latin for 'to make heavier', assuming that an existing condition is made worse). Aggro became so commonly used in the later decades of the 20th century that its meaning widened and weakened: far from describing, say, a potential street fight, it can now be applied to something as minor as being a few minutes late, thus causing aggro to the person waiting.

Q A into G

Either a description of one's own burst of activity, or sometimes an instruction to someone else, to get started, become active, *do* something. It is a polite abbreviation of *arse into gear*.

Q All Blacks

The *New Zealand Encyclopedia* reports that the name All Blacks began in 1905 when the New Zealand Rugby Union team was touring Britain and played in a place called Hartlepool. A British reporter who covered the event wrote that the whole team played as if they were all backs. By a typographical error, this was printed as all blacks.

Other researchers have queried this: nobody, it seems, has ever tracked down the exact newspaper report in which the 'mistake' occurred. Suffice to say that, one way or another, the name All Blacks certainly became a fixture on that 1905 tour and has stuck ever since. And by then, they were wearing black, having started out in 1884 wearing dark blue.

Q Amber liquid

Towards the end of the 20th century, beer began to widen its image in New Zealand. Advertising featured sophisticated people in upmarket foreign localities, drinking beer (sometimes from New Zealand). Before that, beer had been firmly associated with physical activity, contact sports, noise and men. Women seldom drank it. A 'beery party' didn't necessarily refer to what was being drunk, but more to the rambunctious atmosphere the word beer evoked.

Whether through some hangover of temperance puritanism or an uncharacteristic desire to make the language more colourful, beer is often referred to by other names. Rather than say the word itself, suds and sauce were used as informal replacements — and often the noun was dropped altogether. 'To have a few' or 'sink a few' are common New Zealand expressions — the listener mentally adds the word 'beers'.

During the 1970s, a popular weekly television comedy show featured a group of men in a pub, sinking a few. One of them consistently used the quasi-grandiloquent phrase, amber liquid, whenever he referred to his beer and the term quickly went into general popular usage.

Q America's Cup

When it was first raced for in 1851, this famous sailing prize was called the Hundred Guineas Cup. That competition was won by a schooner called *America*. In time, the cup became popularly referred to as America's Cup, with the apostrophe designating that it belonged to the boat of that name. Then 'the' crept in before the title and it became 'the America's Cup'. And that's how the name has stayed.

New Zealanders paid little attention to the America's Cup until 1985 when *KZ3* was launched. Thus prepared, New Zealand first competed for the cup in 1986, won it in 1995 and successfully defended it in 2000.

Q Anglican

The division of Christianity known in some places as Episcopalian, in New Zealand is commonly referred to as Anglican, sometimes Church of England.

Q Ankle-biters

Made prominent by Australian entertainer Barry Humphries, the term is believed to be of New Zealand origin. It refers, often with affection, to small children. An equivalent to rug rats.

Q Anorak

The hip-length waterproof jacket (often hooded) has a basic shape similar to the traditional garment of Greenland Eskimos, whose language gave us the word — *ánorâq*.

Q Antipodes

The word is Greek for 'opposite the feet', and became a northern hemisphere word in common use when referring to New Zealand and Australia.

Before the 1860s, Europeans, when saying antipodes, meant the whole of the southern hemisphere (see Shakespeare's *Much Ado About Nothing*, Act II, scene 1), but with the growth of colonisation in Australia and New Zealand, British people began to refer to Australians and New Zealanders as Antipodeans, with a capital A.

Curiously, this description is never used by the British when referring to South Africans or South Americans. (It also blithely overlooks the fact that New Zealand is *not* opposite Britain; on the globe, New Zealand is opposite Spain.)

And even more curiously, New Zealanders never use the word when referring to Britain (or Spain), though its use in that context would be entirely valid.

Q Anzac

In 1914 Lieutenant-General Sir William Birdwood took command of the Australian and New Zealand Army Corps, which was destined to land at Gallipoli on 25 April 1915. According to military historian Christopher Pugsley, the acronym ANZAC came into being when clerks at Birdwood's headquarters had the letters printed on a rubber stamp used for registering correspondence. New Zealander Sergeant K.M. Little was credited with the initiative. After the word Anzac had been used among the clerks, Major C.M. Wagstaff suggested that the acronym become the telegraphic codeword for the corps. After that, the word spread into widespread use, and was stamped on boxes of stores used at Gallipoli. It also appeared as part of the name of the beach where the first Anzacs landed: Anzac Cove.

The Dardanelles campaign killed 2721 New Zealanders and wounded 4752 others.

Both New Zealand and Australian soldiers marked Anzac Day in 1916. In 1919 the Anzac Day march in London gained the attendance of the Prince of Wales. The concept of Anzac Day went into official legislation in 1920. A parliamentary order forbade the use of the word Anzac in any commercial activity without approval and the date of Anzac Day must remain at 25 April regardless of the day of the week on which it falls.

During subsequent generations the term Anzac has widened to include all Australians and New Zealanders who have given their lives in military service.

Thousands of Kiwis have helped to commemorate the name by baking millions of Anzac biscuits. A recipe for 'Anzac Cakes' was published in 1915. Then a recipe for 'Anzac Crispies' that appeared in 1921 united the ingredients and method which, by 1927, had become known as Anzac biscuits. That recipe, with its key ingredients of golden syrup and rolled oats (coconut and walnuts optional), remains the classic. There have been only occasional variations, such as the 'millennium' chocolate-coated version which had a brief flurry of popularity in 2000.

 Aotearoa

Aotearoa is acknowledged as the Maori name for New Zealand, though not necessarily the country's *original* name — there is scant evidence that Aotearoa pre-dates the name New Zealand.

According to the late Professor Keith Sinclair, it is extremely doubtful that this country had a name at all in the early days of its habitation. Or, after it became inhabited, that Maori had any all-embracing name for the group of islands in which they lived.

Abel Tasman, in 1642, decided to call what he saw of the colony Staten Land, but that only lasted for one year. The words Nieuw Zeeland and Zeelandia Nova had crept onto maps by the mid 1600s and have been there ever since.

When there was a need for Maori people to recognise a name for the country, the customary transliteration was Niu Tireni (which is the only term found in the Treaty of Waitangi; there is no mention there of Aotearoa). Niu Tireni was in fairly common use throughout the latter half of the 19th century.

Sinclair did not believe Aotearoa to be a traditional name at all. It was 1860 before Aotearoa first surfaced in Maori manuscripts and its origins and meaning have never been clear since. William Pember Reeves used the word Aotearoa in his 1898 history and Sir George Grey believed it to be a version of the word that designated the legendary destination of the canoes by which the Maori first travelled to this country many generations before.

 ## A & P show

In 1843, only three years after the signing of the Treaty of Waitangi, the first Agricultural and Pastoral Association was formed, with the intention of improving crops and agriculture and providing exhibitions of livestock and machinery.

By 1908, a parliamentary act incorporated over 100 A & P Associations throughout the country. Although actively involved in all aspects of rural life (such as improving postal, telephone and school services), the associations were non-political and paid increasing attention to holding A & P shows. These splendid rural-based festivals, centred on the exhibition of livestock and produce (often competitively), the latest machinery models, trade displays and educational material, gradually developed to include additional 'fairground' activities so that they became major annual events in communities throughout New Zealand. The annual A & P show has such a high profile in some areas that it is referred to just as The Show. Canterbury, for instance, has Show Week in November.

 ## Aroha

Aroha is Maori for love in all its various shades of meaning: affection, sympathetic warmth, romantic love for a person, all-embracing love for a family and love of a wide group of people, of a nation or a landscape.

Q Arbor Day

Arbor is Latin for tree (which is why the central desert of Australia is called the Nullabor — Latin for no trees). The idea of ensuring that trees be planted on at least one official day each year originated in Nebraska in 1872.

Early European settlers in New Zealand may not have seen much need to follow this custom, since their new land had plenty of trees, but some wisely saw that vegetation being destroyed by settlement must be replaced. First to follow up the thought was Greytown, on the main road from Wellington to Masterton. In July 1890 it declared an Arbor Day and planted pine trees and spruces, with speeches, ceremonials and a concert. Queen Victoria sent her commendation.

In 1892 the New Zealand government did establish an official annual Arbor Day but shifted the date to August. Another change came in 1972 when, to align New Zealand with World Environment Day, the date of the annual Arbor Day was shifted to 5 June.

Q Arthur's Pass

Arthur Dudley Dobson (1841–1934) was the son of surveyor Edward Dobson, and became a surveyor himself. In March 1864 Arthur Dobson found a way from Canterbury to the West Coast, and in 1865, when gold was discovered on the other side of the Southern Alps, Edward Dobson chose his son's route as the main one to the goldfields. The name Arthur's Pass stuck.

Apart from monarchs, it's fairly uncommon for a placename to commemorate a person's *first* name.

Q Arvo

Short for afternoon, arvo is sometimes extended to sarvo, for this afternoon. The abbreviation is Australian, not New Zealand, but has become familiar in both countries. It first reached Australian dictionaries as a recognisable word in 1927.

 # Australasia

The word seems to have arisen from a mistake. Back in 1794 a French word, *Australasie*, seems to have been used occasionally in reference to Australia and Asia.

Over time, the meaning modified, placing less emphasis on Asia and more on 'Australia and its outlying islands', which included New Zealand. By the end of the 19th century, New Zealand had established an identity of its own, so another slight refinement of meaning took place, and Australasia came to signify 'the separate nations of Australia and New Zealand, plus the outlying islands of both countries'.

The word has always had a somewhat edgy connotation, however it is used. New Zealanders have often felt that the term more or less eliminates New Zealand, and that it conveys a link by subtly allying New Zealanders to a more powerful neighbour. By the end of the 20th century the word was used only seldom, and then grudgingly.

 # Avondale spiders

The Avondale spider is not native. It was imported, accidentally of course. During the 1920s, butchers in the Auckland district of Avondale took delivery of a new-fangled gas refrigerator. Soon after it was unpacked, the staff found strange spiders keeping themselves warm near the machinery that drove the appliance. Because they ate flies and bugs, the butchers weren't dismayed about the spider tenants, so encouraged them by leaving out little bits of mince when the premises were closed for business.

During the 1930s those butchery premises were pulled down, and the resident spiders had to go elsewhere. Avondale spiders aren't poisonous, but they make a curious spitting noise when upset. Not nearly as much of a nuisance as some other imports, the Avondale spiders have simply remained as a local curiosity.

Away with the fairies

This term is used to describe a person who dwells in fantasy, daydreams or is promoting a project that does not appear to be based on reality. Sometimes people say 'away with the pixies'. The expression is rather similar to 'his lift doesn't reach the top floor', or 'two sandwiches short of a picnic'. Although the phrase has fairly wide currency universally, lexicographer Harry Orsman seems to place its origin as New Zealand.

B

Q Bach

A weekend or holiday house, usually simple and even makeshift, the bach is sometimes just a very small house without the attributes expected of a more generous establishment — garage, laundry, pantry. The noun is probably a back formation from the verb 'to bach', which means to live like a bachelor who can't cook and cleans and tidies in a rudimentary way. This term is sometimes used because the man lives alone, or sometimes because 'the wife' is away for a time and the family must cope without her. Baching or staying in a bach is often rather less comfortable than being in a well-run household. The word has been in use in New Zealand since the early 20th century, but is not the only word used to describe a weekend or beach house — mainly in the south of the South Island it is called a crib.

(See also **Crib**)

Q Backblocks

Large areas of land for sale or survey are customarily divided into blocks. As far back as 1852 remote land that was clearly a long way from a house, from a settlement or from coastal activity was referred to as a back block. The two words became joined into one and in general use throughout most of the 20th century came to refer to anywhere that was a long way from a city. Sometimes the point was stretched even further and an outlying suburb of a town or a building somewhere in a non-mainstream part of a city would, somewhat derisively, be called the backblocks.

16

Q Bags that

Bags that, which means making a claim ahead of someone else, as if putting it securely in a sack and guarding it as your own, probably originated as a British poaching term. It has developed a peculiar grammatical twist: 'I bag that' (which would be grammatically correct) is never used, but 'I bags that' (which in formal terms is a grammatical no-no) is universally accepted.

Q Bald as a badger

Although most New Zealanders have never seen a badger, they often use this expression, which originates in Britain. It is an abbreviation of the longer phrase, bald as a badger's bum, which developed out of a widespread belief that bristles for shaving brushes and artists' brushes were plucked from that area of the animal.

Also occasionally heard in New Zealand is bald as a coot. The latter is a kind of bird that is not bald but whose white-fronted head gives an impression of baldness. Australians have created a variation on this by saying bald as a bandicoot, which is an alliterative extension of the coot phrase, amusing to the ear but without any real sense. Like badgers, bandicoots aren't at all bald.

Q Bang

This is a brief way of intensifying a statement, as in, he built the shed bang in the middle of the lawn, or, the boss sacked the whole bang lot of them.

Q Barbecue

The practice of cooking meat over a fire has been followed for thousands of years but the word barbecue has been in use, with more or less its current meaning, only since the 18th century. (Poet Alexander Pope used it in 1734.)

There are two theories about how the word arose. Because often a whole animal was cooked over a fire, the French phrase *barbe à queue* — from head to tail — is advanced as a possible origin. Other sources note that natives in Haiti cooked a beast on a framework-grid constructed of strong green branches which could function as a bed when required, or as a support for roasting or smoking meat. They called it by the West Indian word *berbekot*. Spanish travellers and explorers observed this and pronounced it as *barbacoa*.

The word and the grid were taken to North America, and *barbacoa* became the word applied to the grid on which a whole ox was roasted, and gradually gained the spelling barbecue.

Bedstead-grids and whole beasts slowly faded away and butane bottles and hamburger patties moved in. The word also broadened its meaning, so that now barbecue doesn't mean just the outdoor structure on which meat is cooked, or even the food itself, but includes the party gathering around it — a barbecue. New Zealand usage favours the diminutive — a barbie — and eager salespeople abbreviate still further with just BBQ.

 Barber

The particularly cold wind that sometimes affects the Greymouth area and is said to be sharp enough to shave a man.

 Bash

From the old Scottish expression 'on the bash' (which survives in New Zealand in full), meaning a great spree and drinking marathon, a bash is any one of the parties attended while pursuing pleasures of company, alcohol and noise.

Q Bathroom

Once upon a time it meant a room with just a bath in it, and probably a washbasin, but nothing more. The word came into use when New Zealand's actual lavatories were outside the main part of the house (and may have had little or nothing to do with water). When lavatories moved indoors, New Zealanders tended to have them in a tiny room, separate from the bathroom, which still had just a bath in it. Then two developments occurred: first, modern domestic architecture tended to place the lavatory in the same room as the bath — and many people liked it that way; second, there is a very strong reluctance among Americans to say the words lavatory or toilet. When Americans say they are going to the bathroom, they almost invariably mean they are going to use a toilet. (So powerful is this American reluctance, that a New Zealand host asked by her American guest where the bathroom was, innocently sent the guest to the bathroom, which was separate from the lavatory. The guest returned in a state of agitation, and still unable to grasp the nettle, said, 'There's no bathroom in your bathroom.')

Q Because it is there

When asked why he had climbed Mount Everest, Sir Edmund Hillary's reply, 'Because it is there', became quite famous. But the reporter who publicised this answer didn't realise that Hillary was actually quoting an earlier famous mountaineer, George Leigh Mallory, who had first made the remark in 1924.

Hillary had no intention of pretending that he had invented the laconic remark. A mountaineer, surrounded by other mountaineers, all of whom knew the Mallory line, Hillary may have assumed everyone else also knew that he was jokingly quoting the earlier man. Such mistakes often happen: one person quotes another, believing that the remark is recognised, but it isn't, and the attribution becomes muddled.

Mallory's niece, Mrs Newton Dunn, wrote to the *Daily Telegraph* in 1986 and explained that the question had originally been put to Mallory by his own sister (Mrs Dunn's mother) and Mallory's reply was one of impatience, 'because a silly question deserves a silly answer'.

 Beehive

Internationally it means a natural home for bees, but in New Zealand it is also the official name of the Government Office Building. Sir Basil Spence's original design for the building was somewhat jokingly compared to the shape of a beehive and the name stuck. The building is even listed in the Wellington phonebook as the Beehive.

 Bench

In Britain and New Zealand the bench is normally the flat working area in a kitchen or DIY area. In other countries this is customarily called a counter, but New Zealand reserves counter for use only to name the flat space in a shop which divides customer from staff.

 Berm

Most New Zealanders don't recognise this word, yet the *Collins English Dictionary* will tell you it is found mainly in New Zealand, which is true. Berm is the official word (as used by city councils and such-like) for the strip of grass between the footpath and the road, between the boundry of a house and the footpath, or between the boundary and the road, if there is no footpath. Berm is related to brim, both words descending from an ancient Scandinavian word meaning edge. The word berm used to crop up in describing castles, signifying a narrow edge of battlements or moats. But since castle warfare died out, berm appears to have survived only in

New Zealand, although more New Zealanders now seem to say grass verge instead.

Bickies

In New Zealand there are two distinct meanings of the word bickies (sometimes spelt bikkies). First it is (as in many places) a childish abbreviation for biscuits. But late in the 20th century a separate meaning arose: money — usually in large amounts. Whereas *not* having any bickies could simply mean being caught short when you want to buy a snack, the term is more often 'big bickies' — as in a high salary, an impressive lottery win or a fortunate house sale.

The opposite — small bickies — is also possible, though less frequent. But because the association between bickies and money carries a connotation of circumstances and conditions, there are common variants such as stiff bickies and tough bickies (bad luck, or circumstances that are hard to deal with and require endurance).

Biddy-bid

This is a New Zealand native creeping plant with burrs, many-seeded fruits with little hooked spines that get caught in sheep's wool and people's clothing. The English name is a corrupted pronunciation of the Maori name piripiri.

Whatever they're called, biddy-bids are a great nuisance to sheep farmers, since the burrs remaining obstinately in the fleece reduce the wool's value. Even a domestic pet can be seriously bothered by them and cleaning off a tracksuit when its owner has run through a patch is a frustrating job requiring meticulous finger-picking.

Q Bill

In a restaurant, the written-down total cost of the meal is called a bill, just like any other bill showing an amount owing. Exposure to Americanisms has made the curious term 'check' at least recognisable, but most New Zealanders stick to asking for the bill.

(See also **Docket**)

Q Billy

There is a very old Scottish dialect word *billy-pot*, which could be the ancestor of the common Australasian term billy, meaning a cylindrical metal utensil (usually with a lid) used for carrying food or liquid and sometimes used for (outdoor) cooking. Early New Zealanders were also familiar with a type of tinned meat called bouilli, which came in a tin can, often later used for cooking — the meat itself being anglicised into the term bully beef.

A billy (sometimes given its full name billy-tin) was once a common part of a New Zealand household. Milk was collected in it (before bottles or cartons), fruit was gathered in it and water boiled for outside tea-making. This still happens: trampers and hikers and sleepers out-of-doors pack a billy as a natural accessory to the activity. Primitive bread, cakes and stew can be cooked in a billy.

'Boiling the billy' is another way of saying making tea and 'keeping the billy boiling' has extended into vernacular as a way of saying make sure everything keeps going.

Q Birdcage

The term birdcage is customarily used by New Zealanders to describe the parade ring in which horses appear before a race. The term has been used here since the 19th century, and nobody knows why. With the possible exception of Newmarket, the term seems unknown in other racecourses around the world.

The New Zealand use has nothing to do with:

(1) the similarly named observation carriage on early New Zealand trains. (New Zealand racecourses and their birdcages were in action before there were trains), or;

(2) the street in London called Birdcage Walk, which was actually a large collection of caged exotic birds established by Charles II — until the birds all died of cold.

 Biscuit

It is a snack food, normally oven-baked and usually sweet, and always flat. There is no rising or leavening element in its mix and hence no puffiness (that would be a cake). In some other cultures, biscuit tends to describe different kinds of baked goods, sometimes quite puffed-up, and the flat ones can be known as cookies or crackers.

 Bledisloe Cup

London-born Charles Bathurst graduated from Oxford University in 1890. Although called to the bar in 1892, he returned to study from 1893 to 1896 at the Royal Agricultural College, Cirencester. After gaining his diploma there, he returned to the law until 1910 when he entered Parliament and became a champion of British agriculture, working tirelessly with the full support of the farming community. Made a baron in 1918, he was appointed Governor-General of New Zealand in 1929 (he took up office the following year) and excelled in every possible way. It was widely hoped in 1935 that his term would be extended, but Lord Bledisloe returned to Britain.

He left several remarkable legacies. Probably the most important was his private purchase of the land where the Treaty of Waitangi was signed. This property had been owned by James Busby and had gradually deteriorated. Lord Bledisloe and his wife bought it and presented it to the nation in 1932 to be administered by a specific act.

He also donated a splendid cup, for competition in rugby between Australia and New Zealand, first played for in 1931. The winning or losing of it has stirred hearts every year since.

 # Bloke

Somehow, 'bloke' seems to summon up the image of an Australian or New Zealand man, and it is generally in those two countries that you hear the word, though it originally came from the British Isles. In the 18th and 19th centuries, nomadic or itinerant tinkers travelled around fixing up people's pots and pans. They were not an entirely reliable group of people and used to speak to each other in a quasi-language known as Shelta, which was a kind of slightly altered Gaelic. Bloke in that language was an informal word for an ordinary man. The word was used sparingly in Britain and is not common there, but Australians and New Zealanders, in a spirit of egalitarianism, use it frequently. Its feminine form, blokess, seems to have been invented by Jim Hopkins and popularised by the late comedian Billy T. James during the 1970s.

 # Blow that!

An abbreviation of blow that for a joke, this indicates vehement non-agreement, even disgust, certainly dismissal. At times, language substitutes a mild term for an offensive one, and blow that is sometimes thought to be a substitute for damn that (damn still being considered a curse in some countries and very offensive).

There is also an influence from the military descriptions of bombing — blowing up — which indicates that a suggestion is being firmly rejected by the person spoken to, who proposes that the whole idea be blown up, smashed out of use, discarded.

 Bludge

The old word bludgeon meant a heavy stick and the person armed with it was called a bludgeoner. The word is still occasionally used, normally as a verb, when someone is attacked and bludgeoned with a blunt object.

But a bludgeoner, the person demanding obedience, gradually became shortened to bludger, and the meaning softened, particularly in this country. Since approximately 1900 in New Zealand and Australia, a bludger isn't necessarily a person who brandishes a big stick but someone who, much more passively, manages to get other people to do essential things. From this we get the verb 'to bludge', meaning to impose on, to shirk responsibility or hard work, or to borrow excessively, to sponge.

(See also **Cadge**)

Q 'Blue Smoke'

The great Maori singer Ana Hato was recorded in Rotorua in 1927, and June Barson, the New Zealand winner of the worldwide Deanna Durbin contest, was recorded in 1938. But in these and other cases, the actual processing and disc-pressing was done overseas. In 1948 'Blue Smoke', a New Zealand song written by Ruru Karaitiana, became the first-ever performance recorded and processed within New Zealand.

Ruru Karaitiana had been a soldier in the Second World War, and the 'blue smoke' of his song is the smoke drifting homewards towards loved ones as the troopship sails away from New Zealand. Pixie Williams was the singer on the first-ever recording and, 50 years later, her version became available on CD.

Q Bobby calves

The word calf is fairly universal for a young cow or bull and generally means that the creature is up to one year old. But references to bobby calves often confuse visitors to New Zealand. The bobby part of the expression is of British origin: it comes from a dialect term in Cornwall and refers to a very young calf. In New Zealand the term has been widely used in country areas since the 1920s or even earlier. The Ministry of Agriculture defined the term bobby calf in 1982 as a calf that is a minimum of four days old and younger than seven days and has been fed solely on whole milk. Its navel must be dry and it must be able to stand on its own. This definition sets out the guidelines for slaughter.

Bobby calves are generally sold for slaughter. (The secretion rennet, used in cooking to curdle milk, comes only from the stomach of very young calves.)

Bobsy die

The ancient English expression Bob's-a-dying came to mean a great commotion and by 1800 the commotion of Bob's death (whoever that originally was) had shifted from sadness and grief to an expression used by naval men to describe a joyous commotion (often involving some drunkenness).

The phrase went through several changes — Bobs-a-dial, Bobs-a-dilo — before emerging in its probably final form, bobsy-die (or bobsidie).

It still signifies something of a commotion but with various shades of meaning such as being caught in confusion, suffering from upset emotions or simply high-spirited. These uses appear in New Zealand but not noticeably elsewhere.

Bog

Based on an old Gaelic word *bogach*, meaning soft swamp, bog is used in English to describe the same — wet spongy territory, often with decaying matter and equally often with the smell that goes with that.

By the 1800s the word was being used in English as slang for a lavatory, the practice having apparently started at Oxford University. (Sometimes it was used in plural — the bogs — if there were multiple lavatories.) Using the word bog is not uncommon among New Zealanders — even in jocular fashion referring to the pristine marble splendours of an upmarket hotel whose lavatories in no way resemble any midden.

Nearly every culture has this dichotomy regarding lavatories: a formal word and several other informal substitutes. In New Zealand you'll also occasionally hear khasi, jakes, the head, long drop, the can, dubs (short for WC) and dunny (derived from the British dialect word *dunnakin* which is believed to have developed from dung).

(See also **Bathroom, Loo**)

 Boks

The springbok (sometimes spelt springbuck) is an antelope native to southern Africa. Its name harks back to a combination of Dutch words meaning leaping goat. As many sporting teams worldwide adopted the name of animals with admirable qualities, so the South African rugby team was named the Springboks.

New Zealanders' passion for abbreviating whenever possible soon shortened this to the boks (as with the cricketers from West Indies, who by way of the newspaper abbreviation W. Indies, became known in New Zealand as — the Windies).

 Bombay Hills

After the immigrant ship *Bombay* arrived in New Zealand in 1865, most of the passengers collected together in a little settlement 50 kilometres south of Auckland which was then named after the ship. Bombay is on a fairly gentle row of hills that runs roughly east-west across a narrow portion of the North Island.

For many decades, the hills were no big deal to the people who lived around there, and the road going over them, the Razorback, was mentioned far more often. When the Razorback was replaced with a new road — the Deviation — *that* became the common point of reference.

As the city of Auckland grew and stretched towards natural geographic boundaries, the suburbs came almost as far as the Bombay Hills. But the south side of the hills remained noticeably rural. Some citizens of New Zealand's South Island became heavy with scorn about the glitzy lifestyle they imagined Auckland to have and, early in the 1980s, these people began referring to Auckland as 'north of the Bombay Hills' and the rest of New Zealand as 'south of the Bombay Hills'.

Until that expression took hold, most people in Auckland city were unaware there was a place called Bombay on its southern border and even the people who lived nearby seldom referred to the hills by name.

 Bonnet

The lift-up cover over the engine of a car is, in other countries, sometimes called the hood. A New Zealander who needs to look at the car engine will lift up the bonnet, but an American is more likely to pop the hood.

(See also **Boot**, **Mudguard**)

 Bookings

To most New Zealanders it's a simple enough matter: to make a future arrangement for the services of, say, a plumber or a builder, or to ensure a seat in a theatre or on a plane, you make a booking.

This confuses some visitors, who imagine that booking has something to do with reading, or with making bets with a bookmaker. This is because a commonly equivalent term in other cultures is a reservation. You reserve in advance. In essence the two terms mean the same thing and are interchangeable.

Q Boot

Possibly because of its meaning as a protective cover, the word boot became the British name for the storage section of a car which had a separate close-off door. This usage prevails in New Zealand, where the boot of the car has quite a clear meaning, and weekend boot sales are a gathering of cars parked around an open public space, each with its boot open and goods for sale displayed. In the United States that same part of a car is consistently called the trunk, which is equally logical since it means an enclosed box-like container for storing or carrying goods.

Q Boots and all

Often used in the phrase 'to go in boots and all', this expression means to act with a strong sense of purpose, allowing nothing to stand in the way, to be totally committed.

Q Bot (the)

The unpleasant botfly has parasitic larvae which develop inside the bodies of horses and sheep. A beast carrying the (visible) eggs on its surface was said to have the bots and the eggs needed to be scoured off. This familiar rural term eventually narrowed to just the bot or a bot and became universally used to describe human illness, especially that of a temporary kind, caused by infection from someone else afflicted.

Q Bottle store

This is a retail outlet where bottles of liquor can be sold and taken away for drinking elsewhere. But, unlike a wine shop, a bottle store is usually attached to a licensed tavern or hotel. Elsewhere it can be called an off-licence or just a liquor store. Visitors passing a New Zealand bottle store are sometimes confused: 'What do they sell in there? Just empty bottles?'

 Bowser

In the early days of the internal combustion engine, the beast was fed its petrol from a separate upright pump with a long hose. The American firm S.F. Bowser Ltd in Indiana was a prolific manufacturer of these pumps, many of which were used in New Zealand from 1919. The name of the company became widely used to refer to the pump itself, or to the business establishment where one or several of them could be found.

The word bowser stuck for a very long time in Australasia and was perhaps driven out of existence by the growth of fuel companies with aggressive marketing so that the customer was constantly alerted to the brand of petrol being bought, rather than the pump dispensing it (which, strictly, was what a bowser was).

Gradually, bowser became petrol pump and eventually service station (even for those establishments that encourage customers to fill their own tanks, thus not actually providing service).

 **Box of birds**

This popular phrase is believed to have originated in the New Zealand military during the Second World War and was first printed in 1943. Although an actual box of birds might possibly be a miserable sight (think of battery hens), the intention of the expression is to express fitness and happiness. Besides this cheerful image, the phrase also has what etymologists call 'pleasing alliteration', which makes it easy and pleasant to say. Some years later, approximately 1980, the expression was frequently modified into box of budgies, which retained both the alliteration and the cheerfulness. Another variation, a box of fluffy ducks, lost the alliteration but still had a chirping image of youth and eagerness.

Q Bro

Although it is simply an abbreviation of brother, the term bro has a wider set of meanings within New Zealand. Maori families often contain what, in formal terminology, would be called a foster child, a stepchild, a half-sibling or even a legal cousin. Referring to that person as a bro can establish that there is a close link of upbringing but not necessarily a strict blood relationship.

The term widens considerably when used to refer to other (Maori) members of an affiliate group, such as a gang, who are all bros to each other in spirit.

Even more widely, it is sometimes heard somewhat ironically or humorously to refer to Maori people in general who, because of affiliation by race, are all bros.

(See also **Cuzzie**)

Q Buckshee

It usually means free of any monetary charge or an unexpected extra beyond the expected. Since it came into use during the First World War, the word has appeared in various spellings — mainly because it was picked up by military personnel from hearing the Arabic word *baksheesh*, meaning a gift or a present. In a wartime context buckshee also carried an important secondary meaning: a slight wound that did not cause major damage but merited being shipped home from the front. This latter reference became less common in peacetime but the meaning 'free' remains common.

Q Buddy

Derived from a baby-talk version of brother, the word is widely used in the United States to mean friend and can frequently be heard in New Zealand, usually describing a fairly light form of friendship (school buddies, sports buddies) rather than a person with whom one has a long-lasting association. That person is more

usually called a mate.
  (See also **Mate**)

 Bugger

Bugger started out as a clandestine word but not a dirty one. Centuries ago, some citizens of Bulgaria took up religious sects that mainstream Europe didn't approve of, so on some occasions the word Bulgarian was used to mean a group of mavericks or weirdos, outsiders.

The word caught on and when it drifted into English, as bugger, it still meant outsiders, but not necessarily religious ones: it came to signify homosexual male partners. Gradually the word extended into a more general exclamation of surprise, shock or vehement irritation. But in any of its uses, bugger was still regarded as vulgar usage and was discreetly kept away from most public arenas.

In 1999 a New Zealand television commercial took the word, in its exclamation of irritation mode, right into everyone's home and, in spite of some protests, made it comically acceptable.

There are various expansions on bugger. Bugger-lugs is a fairly common sobriquet, based on an old-time nautical expression that was not necessarily offensive; bugger off means go away; bugger up is to confuse or render inoperative; bugger all is a small amount, insufficient, not enough; bugger that — I don't like it; and bugger me — I'm surprised.

 Bull

Although bull obviously means the male dairy animal, it also often occurs as an abbreviation to indicate some affiliation with that animal's products, as in bulldust (nonsense), bull-artist (someone who tells unbelievable stories) and, of course, bullshit (indicating that the matter under discussion is beneath contempt).

Bumper

The horizontal bar at the back and front of a vehicle which protects against accidental impact damage. Other people sometimes call it a fender.

(See also **Mudguard, Boot, Bonnet**)

Bun fight

Not a specifically New Zealand expression but one that may have fallen into disuse elsewhere, since it always seems to amuse visitors who hear New Zealanders say it.

A bun fight is any sort of social function at which food is also available (it is not the main reason for the occasion). Although it is usually said in a spirit of fun, there are those who consider it smart to use the term as a deliberate put-down by referring to the grandest possible function, say a reception by the Governor-General, as a bun fight at Government House.

Bung

To be bung is to be broken, not functioning as desired. It comes from an Australian Aboriginal dialect word (from Yagara, in the Brisbane area) meaning dead.

Bungy

There are various spellings — bungy, bunjie and bungee. The word seems to have started life as injie, an informal name for a pencil eraser made of India rubber. Most of these rubbers were short and thick, so the word drifted towards bunjie or bungy because of how they felt — short and thick, like a barrel bung. The word also surfaced as Navy slang for a physical training instructor. Possibly because all these elements involved bounciness, during the mid-20th century the word began to describe strong rubbery-elastic cords with a hook at each end which were used to secure baggage (and packages onto a bicycle).

By 1980 the term bungy cords (or bunjie cords or bungee cords — take your pick) was being applied to much longer straps attached to people's ankles when they jumped (quite voluntarily) from high places, then bounced back up.

This voluntary high-jumping, with restraining cords preventing impact, originated as a manhood ritual in Pentecost Island, Vanuatu, where young males jumped from high tree-platforms using ropes made of flexible jungle creepers. The humble origins of the activity have become highly sophisticated in modern bungy jumping, which has been streamlined into a money-making enterprise involving complex bungy ropes or restraining gear, and jump-offs as exotic as the Eiffel Tower.

(There is no connection with failing to perform or going bung, which is an Australian term derived from the Aboriginal word for dead.)

Burl (or Berl or Birl)

The word is frequently heard, as in give it a burl, but the origin is unclear. It may be a variation on either hurl or whirl but it also may be derived from an old British dialect word meaning spin. To give it a burl usually means to give something a try or, better, attempt an activity that may be difficult but that one is courageous enough to tackle.

There is also a vague connection with the fishing term burley, which is a common New Zealand name for bait spread on water. That word is thought to originate from an Australian expression meaning nonsense, rubbish (burley fish-bait is hardly elegant), or that, in spreading out this mess, you are trying to catch fish, in other words, giving it a burl.

Bush

Derived from the Dutch word *bosch*, meaning woodland, this is the preferred New Zealand word for territory that is heavily treed. There is a resistance to the more English 'woods' (that somehow suggests clear space around the bases of the trees, which New Zealand bush doesn't usually have) or the rather more grand 'forest', which is used in New Zealand to describe areas of exotic trees that have been deliberately planted, as well as those growing naturally. If a treed area is especially large and distinctly native, it might be called native forest, but if you call it bush or the bush you will still be understood.

(See also **Go bush**)

Bush lawyer

New Zealand native versions of the blackberry vine have acquired the popular name bush lawyer, probably from an English dialectical use of the same term, indicating that the thorns of the vine are as difficult to escape as the entanglements of the legal system.

When referring to a person rather than a plant, the term bush lawyer has two levels of figurative meaning: (a) a lawyer who involves someone in a legal complexity from which it is difficult to escape, or (b) a non-qualified person who, simply from observing the process of law, claims to have knowledge and is ready to give opinions on legal matters. The second meaning is the most widely used.

Buzzy Bee

Two Auckland brothers named Hec and John Ramsey were designers and manufacturers of very charming toys. Peter Pup, Richard Rabbit and Playful Puss were popular examples. In 1947 they launched a new example: a fat, surprised-looking wooden bee, with little wheels and a string to drag it along the floor. A simple stroke of near-genius gave the toy a supreme attraction for young children — the wheels not only made the wings go round, but also activated an internal metal strip that made a noise. It did not really sound much like a bee — it was more of a clack-clack — but it delighted little kids.

One of those inexplicable miracles of market consciousness took place: the Buzzy Bee became a standard feature in almost every New Zealand family home. The pup, the rabbit and the puss were all but forgotten, but the Buzzy Bee was everywhere.

In the decades since, the Buzzy Bee has acquired icon status as an amusing and unique product of New Zealand inventiveness. Its acceptance into respectability was probably confirmed when, during a royal visit, the infant Prince William seized one and gleefully dragged it across a mat under the frantic lenses of gathered international press.

The bee's name was not patented until 1975 and within 10 years its manufacture had quietly shifted to China, but it remains very much part of New Zealand folklore.

Q BYO

The expression started out in the late 1950s as BYOG — bring your own grog — and was appended to party invitations, especially university events. Such was its transparent simplicity that very quickly the G was lost, since everyone knew what you were supposed to bring.

By the late 1960s the initials began to appear on restaurant signs, indicating that the business was not licensed to sell liquor, but was able to serve alcohol brought in by a customer who was eating there. (New Zealand law did not allow restaurants to sell alcohol until 1961.)

The expression BYOG is related to a similar phrase heard in some other countries PBAB — please bring a bottle.

Cabbage trees

The tall tree *Cordyline australis* is one of the most characteristic and familiar sights in the New Zealand landscape. It is not quite so familiar in Britain: one town there that boasts a grove of imported New Zealand cabbage trees relentlessly describes them as palms, which they're not.

In pre-European days, Maori people steamed and baked the main root of the cabbage tree to make a nutritious meal. A sugary substance in the root structure crystallises during the cooking process, and makes the vegetable very palatable (though the process of digging up the root probably destroys the tree).

As early as 1769, European visitors, then later settlers, removed the soft young leaves from the centre of the tree's head, and cooked them as a substitute for cabbage — which gave the tree its popular English name — though a 1773 report said some sailors thought the taste was more like sweet fresh almonds.

Foreign tourists, who see cabbage trees every day while in New Zealand, sometimes query why they never see the leaves on a menu. Perhaps it is because 'real' cabbages became freely available in New Zealand late in the 19th century.

 Cadge

Since the 17th century this word has simply meant to borrow, but it has developed an unspoken sub-text, along the lines of borrowing something because you haven't made the effort to organise yourself properly.

(See also **Bludge**)

Q Capping

This is the ceremony which marks the fact that a person has satisfied all requirements for a degree from a university or other tertiary institution and has thus become a graduand. The hatless graduand is presented with a certificate marking his or her achievement. At that point the graduand puts on a traditional mortar board hat and becomes a graduate. (The mortar board hat is also sometimes called a trencher.) The entire ceremony is customarily referred to by either name: graduation or capping.

It is possible to graduate without undergoing the ritual of wearing a mortar board — simply by receiving your diploma through the mail — but it is not possible to participate in a capping ceremony unless you are eligible to graduate.

In New Zealand, the term graduation applies only to tertiary qualifications. In general, pupils do not graduate from secondary schools.

Q Caravan

Originally a Persian word (*karwan*), the term described a group of traders or travellers, covering long distances with wagons, mules or horses, almost always in single file.

When the word went into English as caravan, it retained its original meaning when used in a suitable context, but developed a secondary and less exotic meaning: an enclosed carriage with some home comforts, not equipped with its own motor, but able to be towed behind a vehicle.

New Zealanders use the word in exactly that sense but could be met with a blank stare if they say it to an American. In that country a caravan is called a trailer, which confuses a New Zealander for whom a trailer is a smallish, open-topped, tray-shaped structure, towed behind a car and piled high with camping gear or garden refuse.

The bastion of New Zealand summer holidays at a beach — the caravan site — in the United States is called a trailer park and may contain many trailers where people live more or less permanently.

Nor is the trailer/caravan to be confused with an American mobile home, which is totally different — it has a motor, and can be lived in and driven from place to place. New Zealanders would call this a campervan.

Carbonettes

Heavily compressed dry carbon fuel roughly in the shape of hens' eggs, in some places these are also called brickettes. They are a dying breed because their only use is in a fireplace, and fireplaces are a dying breed.

Cardigan Bay

Cardigan Bay is a place in Wales, but for New Zealanders the name refers to a very famous racehorse. Cardigan Bay was born in Mataura, near Gore, in 1956 and had spectacular successes. Once when he competed in the Auckland Cup he was handicapped over 70 yards behind the start, but he still won. Americans bought Cardigan Bay, and he raced in the United States with great distinction, becoming the first horse to win a total of US$1 million. His sale contract included a clause saying that, when retired, he must be brought back to New Zealand. This happened, and the beautiful horse lived for some stately years on Sir Henry Kelliher's private island, Puketutu, near Auckland. When he died in 1988, he was buried at the entrance to the Auckland Trotting Club. Many Kiwis referred to him fondly as Cardy.

 Cardy

Sometimes also written as cardie, cardy is an abbreviation of cardigan, a knitted coat-like outer garment, usually long-sleeved and either buttoned or zipped up the front.

In 1854, James Thomas Brudenell, the Earl of Cardigan, was largely responsible for developing a buttoned knitted coat with no collar, which he wanted to wear in the Crimean War. This was thought to be the first-ever knitted outer garment made of wool. Known initially as the Cardigan Bodywarmer, it was only worn by men. (Women did not commonly wear knitted outer garments until the beginning of the 20th century.) In time the garment's name shortened to just cardigan, it was modified for women to wear (especially during the First World War) and its sleeve length was adjusted to be either long or short.

In spite of the garment's popularity, its name, and particularly the abbreviation cardy, developed a pejorative connotation. Merely mentioning that a person wore a cardy summoned an instant image of lack of style and class, though the garment itself was completely acceptable in, say, a twin set.

Variations on the original name — such as cardigan jacket, knit jacket or cardigan sweater — attempt to soften the slightly unwelcome sound of the word cardigan, but the basic garment these words describe is still widely worn, and is still essentially the same as that invented by Lord Cardigan.

The abbreviation cardy did not originate in this country, but lexicographer Harry Orsman says it has 'high frequency use within New Zealand'.

 Carpet

As in Britain, in New Zealand carpet means a large amount of floor covering, usually fixed in place and unable to be moved without difficulty. A rug, on the other hand, is a small independent piece of floor covering that can easily be lifted and moved from place to place. (Sometimes a very large rug, which covers a whole room, but is moveable, can be referred to as a carpet. It seems to be the mobility of the item that determines the name.)

Americans usually say rug to describe all carpeting, no matter how large or permanent. In a slight reversal of the New Zealand usage, American carpet is something mobile and not extensively wide, for example the red carpet rolled out when a VIP leaves a plane.

Descriptive American terms such as shag rug can raise a New Zealand eyebrow (it means having a heavy or floppy pile on the surface), such as the sign seen in dry-cleaning windows: 'Shag rugs cleaned here'.

Confusingly, Americans also commonly say rug to mean hairpiece or toupee.

 ## Cattle-stop

A metal grid covering a ditch, usually at a farm gateway, so that animals such as cattle and sheep cannot pass through, but vehicles and pedestrians can. Hooved animals cannot negotiate the gaps between the narrow horizontal rails.

 ## Caucus

In general, it is believed that New Zealand's parliamentary structure is based on the Westminster system. To a large extent this is true, but there have been influences from other sources. For instance, the meeting of the parliamentary members of a political party in order to co-ordinate policy, known as a caucus, has little to do with Westminster.

Caucus is a fairly rare example of a Native American Indian word in general use in New Zealand. It comes from the Algonquin tribe where the word *caucauas* meant adviser or counsellor. The anglicised version of the word has been in use in the United States since the mid-1600s and in New Zealand since 1876.

Cervena

This is a trade name for New Zealand deer-meat that has been raised on a farm rather than caught in the wild (that meat is venison). The word was invented in 1993 after 4000 other words were considered. The 'cer' comes from *Cervidae*, the Latin for deer, the 'ven' is a reference to venison and the final 'a' is a gesture towards A-grade.

 Chateau cardboard

Bulk wine, often known as quaffing wine, and lacking elegant ancestry, is sold in cardboard boxes with a plastic lining. During the 1970s, some wit coined the term Chateau cardboard and radio personality Sharon Crosbie catapulted the expression into national fame.

 Cheeky

When Fred Astaire sang about dancing cheek to cheek everyone knew what he meant, but cheek and cheeky have another very common meaning in New Zealand: impertinent, bold, saucy, impudent. Some cultures might use such words as sassy, chutzpah or gall. In New Zealand cheeky could describe an over-talkative child, a quaint poster, a boldly designed dress or (stretching things a bit) a perky-tasting wine.

Q Cheerio

A very small savoury sausage, usually bright red and often served in a pile on trays with a collection of toothpicks to help eat them one by one, and a bowl of tomato sauce in which to dip them. Visitors from the United States are sometimes confused because, for them, Cheerios are a well-known sugary breakfast cereal (named for the wheat-producing Cerignola district of Italy).

These miniature spiced sausages aren't a New Zealand invention, but the name is. In other countries they're called simply cocktail sausages, maybe wieners or weenies, and Australia calls them little boys. But the word Cheerios was registered in 1933 as a New Zealand trademark for the little sausages in this country.

Chemist

A shop at which medical prescriptions can be made up (by a qualified pharmacist, or chemist) and which also sells potions, pills and powders directly to do with the body, e.g. shampoos, headache tablets, suntan lotion, cosmetics, etc. Normally they do not sell food or edible goodies, unlike an American drugstore, which often sells just about everything, including fizzy drinks and ice creams, but might not have a qualified chemist to make up prescriptions. You'll more likely find that person at a druggist, which is marginally different.

Chesdale cheese

In 1968, Butland Industries asked Dormer Beck Advertising to create a commercial for their Chesdale processed cheese. The advertising men found, somewhat to their surprise, that many people perceived processed cheese as just various bits and kinds of cheese all flung together. This was not the case, however: Chesdale was actually a good cheddar cheese, especially made for processing.

Illustrator Dick Frizzell was involved in creating the characters of Ches and Dale, two farmers, whose words made it clear that Chesdale was, in fact, 'finest cheddar, made better'.

With a jaunty tune by musician Terry Gray and splendid animation, the Ches and Dale commercial was launched on television in 1968 (in black and white). Such was its success that, for at least 30 years, there was hardly a New Zealander who didn't know the song.

On one classic occasion, a New Zealand government delegation at an overseas forum found themselves required to sing a 'national folk song' at the closing social function. Unable to think of something suitable, they sang:

> We are the boys from down on the farm,
> We really know our cheese
> There's much better value in Chesdale,
> It never fails to please.
> Chesdale slices thinly,
> Never crumbles, there's no waste
> And boy, it's got a mighty taste.
> Chesdale cheese:
> It's finest Cheddar, made better.

Chicken and chook

The word chicken used to conjure up exactly what it meant: an image of a fluffy little creature, recently emerged from a shell and still coming to terms with the world. Later, that little ball of feathers would grow into a hen or a fowl.

But the marketing need to make all flesh sound quick-cook, young and tender caused the lines to blur and the meaning of chicken stretched upwards to include rather more mature candidates. It's hard to justify the accuracy of calling a size 16 bird weighing 1.5 kilograms a chicken.

Gradually, chicken replaced the words hen and poultry. People used to keep hens; now they're all called chickens. Hen is almost archaic and anyone wanting to buy a boiling fowl would probably have to explain.

Chook and chookie are British vernacular terms for chicken closely related to the dialect term of affection 'chuck', which derives from the same source and is often heard in regional speech such as that on *Coronation Street*.

New Zealanders have called their hens chooks for decades. The word described any group of domestic hens, regardless of their various ages and the cry 'Chook-chook-chook' was a familiar rural or suburban sound when feeding time came and the hens rushed forward. (In Australia a prominent politician referred to his press conferences as 'feeding the chooks'.) Sometimes the term was extended past life into the oven — and roast chook would be served.

Because domestic hens have small heads and often seem to behave irrationally, the term 'silly as a chook' still survives.

Chilly bin

For many years it's been known that insulation keeps both warmth and cold inside a prescribed space, therefore someone finally got round to inventing an insulated container in which articles that needed to be kept cold (usually food) could be transported from one place to another without the need for electricity or refrigerants.

The most usual manifestation was a lightweight oblong chest with generous polystyrene lining. Immensely popular for picnics and days at the beach, these were sold in New Zealand under the name Chilly Bin, a trademark registered by Skellerup Industries in 1974. Very soon the trade name became an ordinary word and, like vaseline, nugget and jandal, it went into the language.

Across the Tasman, manufacturers in Australia called their version an Eskie.

Chip

(1) Pieces of chopped potato that have been deep-boiled in fat and are eaten hot. Sometimes called French fries (though they are not French and not fried).

(2) Very thinly sliced potatoes deep-boiled in fat, sealed in air-tight bags and eaten cold — sometimes also known as crisps.

(3) A small and insubstantial container, meant to hold a portion of berry fruits during brief transport.

(See also **Crisps** and **Pottle**)

Q Choice

If something meets with approbation it can be described as neat, cool or choice. Sometimes the meaning can be deliberately ironic, such as describing a particularly unpleasant event as choice when everyone knows that the opposite is intended.

Q Chokka

The ancestor of chokka is the expression chock-full, which itself dates back to the 17th-century term *choke-full*. There is also a relationship with the seamen's term chock-a-block, which refers to a rope passing through a nautical block, but the choke connection is much older. During the 20th century military personnel adopted the term chokka to mean disgruntled, often accompanied by a hand gesture indicating up to here, thus still meaning full.

In New Zealand chokka means full. It sometimes also occurs as chocker or chockers.

Q Chuck

The most common meaning of chuck in New Zealand is throw. For many decades it was regarded as a slang or childish word, not used by adults or educated people. As of 2001, however, it appears in newspapers: the *New Zealand Herald* of 18 May that year reported that a British politician had an egg chucked at him. Some extensions are: chuck off — make fun of; chuck up — to vomit; chuck it in — to relinquish, give up; chuck away or chuck out — to get rid of, throw somewhere else (sometimes stated as 'give it the chuck'). In the United States, chuck describes a cut of steak, and sometimes means beef (or food) in general.

Q Chuddy

This somewhat casual and usually juvenile word for chewing gum came into common usage at the beginning of the 20th century and began to fade from use approximately 100 years later. It was sometimes said in full — chuddygum — and is believed to be a rather loose adaptation of the parent term, chewing gum, or possibly its past participle, chewed.

Because of the importance of the kauri gum industry during New Zealand's earlier days, the word gum meant tree gum. As kauri gum lessened in importance, the American abbreviation for chewing gum — just gum — began to move in and replace the term chuddy.

Q Chuffed, Chuff

To be chuffed in New Zealand means to be pleased, stoked with emotion, filled with joy or pride. The exact origin of the word is much disputed, though one strong candidate is from the 16th century: chuff, which described fat cheeks.

But it is a word to use with care when in British territory where it has two distinct meanings, exactly the opposite of each other.

Fat cheeks can, after all, be puffed from pride and happiness, or inflated with anger. During the 16th and 17th centuries, being chuffed changed meaning from pleased to displeased and then changed back again. From the late 19th century it seems to have settled into meaning pleased. But if there is an old-timer lurking who announces that he or she is chuffed, it might be best to steer clear, because the meaning may not be certain.

In the meantime, the fat cheeks part of the word's history settled into New Zealand and stayed on, but referring to cheeks further south than those on the face. To a New Zealander, chuff by itself means bottom, as in the admonition against laziness: 'Get off your chuff'.

Q Clapped out

The term was in use among London club cyclists in the 1920s, referring to the fact that the riders (not the bikes) were exhausted. Its origin is thought to be totally scurrilous, namely that the person in question was sexually incapacitated as a result of the clap (venereal disease).

During the Second World War the term was spread wide by the RAF, but its meaning shifted away from people and onto machines — aircraft that were no longer serviceable or cars fit only to be sent for scrap. After 1945 clapped out became a general term for anything or anyone who had reached the end of their effectiveness.

Q Claytons

During 1980, New Zealanders were bemused by TV commercials for an Australian drink called Claytons, a richly flavoured non-alcoholic beverage. In the mysterious way in which such things happen, while many other TV commercials vanish from consciousness five minutes after they're viewed, the punchline of this particular ad caught on, and became a national catchphrase: 'Claytons — the drink I have when I'm not having a drink'.

Very quickly the drink's name began to be used when expressing a disillusion that something was not what it seemed to be. By 1983 the nation's annual Budget was being dubbed 'a Claytons Budget' because commentators thought it was not sufficiently connected to reality.

The drink itself faded from prominence very quickly, but the word Claytons was still in use 20 years later as an adjective, indicating that something was a pretence, or an unconvincing imitation of the real thing.

Q Clobber

Although an Englishman might occasionally refer to his clothes as clobber, a New Zealander would rarely do so. But either might mean something quite different by the word: to be beaten up, or beaten down.

In this sense clobber is an old English word, believed to have developed as an echoic form — the word somehow makes a sound that reflects the action of beating. The terms clobber and clobbering were used by the RAF to describe a heavy bombing, and in the Navy to refer to armed submarines successful with their targeting.

Within its meaning of being beaten into submission, clobbering developed a particular metaphoric use in New Zealand, referring to situations where people were expected to conform with accepted standards, rather than display individuality. British author Austin Mitchell, while briefly resident in New Zealand in the 1970s, popularised the phrase 'the Great New Zealand Clobbering Machine', referring to the suppressing qualities of local and bureaucratic conservatism.

Q Clout

The ancient Dutch word *kluit*, meaning a lump, gravitated into English in the 1400s and became clout, which evolved into several different meanings, including a blow with the hand or a hard object, a thump. This meaning has remained firm but in the mid-20th century it began to take on a figurative connotation: because giving a clout implied physical power, the word gradually became a synonym for power. In this guise it is usually preceded by the verb 'to have': a person who has clout is one with some kind of influence, usually concerning local or national politics.

Lesser meanings of the word in British speech (a rag, a garment or to steal) have not gained currency in New Zealand at all, but a sporting celebrity or a financial board member is often described as having clout.

Q Cobber

Cobber is generally thought of as an Australasian word, but there is a similar old dialect word in Britain, cob, meaning to take a liking to someone. Some scholars believe that Australians imported this word from Britain and then expanded it to cobber, meaning a mate.

New Zealanders borrowed it fairly quickly: the word cobber was in print in New Zealand by 1897 and the New Zealand troops in the First World War said it frequently.

Q Coconuts

Coconuts have nothing to do with cocoa. Watch out for the spelling: cocoa with the 'a' comes from a South American native word *cacao*, the name of the plant whose seeds are ground into chocolate powder known as cocoa.

But coconut is quite a different word — it comes from the Portuguese word *coco*, which means grinning face. Look at one end of a fresh coconut and you'll see why they got the name.

When said about Pacific Island people, *coconut* is a term that varies from high goodwill to high insult. In general it would be wise not to risk saying it at all — even if Pacific Islanders use it in a jocular way to describe themselves. That's different.

Q Colonial goose

When British pioneer settlers made the long journey to start a new life in 19th-century New Zealand, they brought all their nursery rhymes with them, including 'Christmas is a-coming and the goose is getting fat'. The idea of roast goose at Christmas was built into the immigrants' psyche, but there were no geese in New Zealand at the time — and if there had been, they wouldn't have been getting fat in December. Somewhat to the new New Zealanders' dismay, Christmas came in summer. It took well over

100 years to adjust to this climatic eccentricity. Hot Christmas meals, fake snow and Dickensian cards showing carollers in the cold have continued to be the norm.

Unwilling to abandon the habit of preparing a Christmas goose, settlers evolved a new antipodean version: boned mutton, filled with savoury stuffing, roasted and served with potatoes. It has nothing to do with geese at all, but the name sounded more Christmassy than stuffed mutton, so colonial goose kept people happy for many decades.

 ## Come again?

This is a very common New Zealand expression which simply means 'Please repeat what you have just said,' sometimes with the added connotation, 'and explain it more clearly'.

 ## Come away

Nymphs and shepherds do not feature in this very common New Zealand term which, instead, means the plants will grow. It is usually applied hopefully to seeds that have been planted, seedlings that are visible and larger shrubs, trees and climbers that have been pruned. They will come away, meaning, grow larger, up into the air!

 ## Compere

Side by side with the equivalent term master of ceremonies, the term compere is widely used in New Zealand to describe the person who introduces the various sections of an event, commentates on happenings, and announces guest speakers etc. The word is completely unknown in some other places, such as the United States, where master of ceremonies or MC has been refined into an entirely new word, emcee.

 Contractor

The same linguistic framework that gives us employ*er* (the person who organises and pays the workforce) and employ*ee* (someone who works for and is paid by an employer) gives us contract*or* (the person initiating the project and paying those working on it) and contract*ee* (who guarantees work to the contractor in return for money). Curiously, the New Zealand vocabulary has more or less abandoned contractee and quite commonly refers to both the person paying out the money and the person earning the money as contractors. This can be slightly confusing since the terminology doesn't make clear who's in charge.

 Cootie

A cute-sounding word that isn't cute at all: it means head-lice, adapted from the Maori word *kutu*.

Corker

Use of this word goes back a long way (you'll find it in P.G. Wodehouse), but its origin is obscure. It seems to have nothing to do with corks and is now rarely used except in New Zealand, where it was first seen in print in 1862, and Australia.

Something which is corker (adjective) or a corker (noun) is estimable, outstanding and remarkable, possibly even desirable. Occasionally the qualifier 'beauty' precedes it: a beauty corker is especially remarkable and worthy of praise.

Q Corrugated iron

New Zealand cannot claim corrugated iron. It was invented in London in 1828 when zinc-coated iron sheets were first put through rollers, causing a series of regular ridges and hollows that conveyed maximum strength. The product became useful in roofs and for farm buildings, but was not confined to those — the royal castle of Balmoral has a ballroom made from corrugated iron.

Such a large amount of corrugated iron is highly visible in New Zealand that it intrigues tourists from places who use very little of it. Whole buildings are made of it (world-famous scientist Lord Rutherford began studying physics and chemistry in an all-corrugated-iron lecture hall at university in Christchurch), as are fences, watertanks and even artworks: grazing cows made from corrugated iron are a splendid sight.

 Cot

The Hindi word *khat*, meaning bedstead, gives us the English word for a lightweight bed, often a small one and especially designed for a baby. The baby's cot is a standard feature of almost every New Zealand household, though in other places this high-sided, padded structure is often called a crib. Retaining the connection with beds, the expression cot-case means that a person is, or should be, confined to bed for reasons of health or exhaustion.

 Cow cockies

There's a cheeky sort of sound to the word cocky, and we'd like to think it was a New Zealand word for a Kiwi farmer — energetic, confident and capable. But no, the expression originates across the ditch in Australia: it's short for cockatoo. (Actually, the word cockatoo isn't Australian anyway — it's derived from Dutch and Malaysian — but by the 19th century the word was well settled into Oz.) When Australians of the city kind observed their country cousins working in the Australian outback, which is often fairly bleak, they were reminded that, like cockatoos, farmers preferred open spaces.

In this country, we only ever seem to hear of cow cockies. This isn't always the case in Australia. Farming has diversified, and with this comes the occasional mention of goat cockies or deer cockies. Other variations haven't caught on in New Zealand, where just saying cocky always means a dairy farmer.

Q Creek

Creek is a very old word that came into English from ancient Dutch *kreke*, but its meaning has diverged. Both *kreke* and its Norse derivative, *kriki*, meant an inlet or a bay, and that was the meaning the word took in English.

Captain Cook probably meant a little harbour when he secured his boat in a creek. But for some odd reason, British settlers to America in the 17th century started using the word to mean a running stream or small river. A century later, immigrants to Australia used the word in that same way, to refer to a freshwater tributary. By the early 19th century, this river usage was also established in New Zealand.

In parts of this country, creek can sometimes be found still referring to a small inlet, but in general it is the word of choice for anything smaller than a river. If very small, a waterway is called a small creek, often in preference to more gentle British words such as rivulet, stream, rill, burn or beck.

Q Crib

Used with strict loyalty in some areas, the word crib describes a weekend or holiday house of fairly simple proportions and facilities. Originally, crib is derived from the ancient German *krebe* meaning basket (the modern German word is *Korb*).

Moving through to Anglo-Saxon, the word became crib in English, with various meanings centred around smallish confined spaces: a child's bed, a cattle stall, cheating by stealing someone else's work (presumably by carrying it away surreptitiously in a little basket!) and a little cottage.

This latter meaning travelled to New Zealand with early

immigrants, and settled itself into the South Island in the late 1800s where it remains firmly in use to describe a (usually rural) cabin or a holiday retreat — something less than a real house. Those who come into a district for a temporary stay in their holiday cottage are sometimes referred to by local permanent residents as cribbies.

Elsewhere in New Zealand the same thing is called a bach. It is one of the few examples of word usage having a distinct variation from one region to another.

(See also **Bach**)

 # Crikey dick

It would seem that, in moments of passionate anger, surprise, shock or despair, people have long wanted to exclaim loudly the name of one major religious figure or another. But the desire to blaspheme is also often tempered by a consciousness that to do so might offend others (and possibly also score a black mark against the oath-maker by some heavenly scorekeeper). Hence the development of similar-sounding words one could say with impunity, such as 'Oh my goodness!', which replaces 'Oh my God!' People would still know what you meant, but no offence was caused.

Crikey, like its cousin, cripes, is a simulation of the word Christ. Gee and jeepers substitute for Jesus, golly and by golly substitute for God (along with their Maori version, pai kori) and, on the other side of the spiritual coin, dickens became a stand-in for the Devil — in such terms as 'what the dickens!'

The expressions originate in Britain but are more frequently heard in New Zealand, where locals frequently invoke the higher and the lower power simultaneously: the expression crikey dick is a socially acceptable euphemism for Christ *and* the Devil.

Q Crisps

Throughout the world there is some variance about the names given to cooked potatoes. In New Zealand, the thinly sliced potatoes pre-cooked in fat, salted, packaged in foil or cellophane and then eaten cold, are sometimes called crisps and sometimes chips, though the latter are more usually freshly cooked and served hot.

Q Crispy

Crisp is an adjective describing something that is fresh, firm and brittle, or orderly and neat, concise and pithy. It comes from the Latin *crispus* meaning curled. During the 17th century, a parallel word, crispy, also existed, meaning much the same thing: curly, wavy, crinkly, brittle or brisk. But for some unknown reason, the word crispy almost vanished from use, and in its various contexts, crisp served the English language quite efficiently for several hundred years. Then an American breakfast cereal company reasoned that their food might seem more attractively snap-crackle-and-pop if described as crispy, so along came Crispy Critters, a breakfast cereal in the shape of animals.

Although the word was not at all new, in New Zealand it seemed cute and was taken up joyously by food writers and television cooks and from 1960 onwards virtually replaced the similar adjective, crisp. According to the food literati, nothing now is ever crisp — it is crispy.

Q Crook

The ancient Norse word *krokh*, meaning a hook, gave English the word crooked and various associated meanings such as a shepherd's crook (hook-shaped) and crook-back (bent out of usual shape). This latter image eventually caused the word crooked to be applied to dishonest people, then shortened to crook.

In New Zealand, by the early years of the 20th century, crook developed many meanings covering a rather wide spectrum: dishonest or financially shady or unkind fortune (a crook deal); unpleasant (a crook party or a crook day); being ill (feeling crook); disturbed (a crook night); badly constructed (crook roof); dishonest (a crook partner); inedible (crook food); anger (to go crook); deterioration (going crook); or bad advice (to put someone crook).

Cuppa

Quite simply, cuppa is short for cup of tea but the meaning extends far beyond the simple beverage and can indicate a work break, socialising, a rest of some sort and very likely some snack-food as well as the actual tea. In a Maori context, being asked to a cuppa after some formal ceremony could involve groaning tables piled high with food.

Cuzzie

This word is a descendant of the old English informal term coz, meaning cousin (Shakespeare uses it). When Europeans first began to settle in New Zealand in the mid-19th century, they were, by reasons of distance, largely isolated from relations who were once removed or twice removed, so New Zealanders lost touch with these minutiae of bloodline and have never taken to them much since. But they continued to adhere to the simpler forms of aunt, uncle, cousins and in-laws.

Maori were largely unfamiliar with some of the basic structures by which European relationship was measured. Extremely knowledgeable about aristocratic succession and their own form of lineage, in closer domestic situations they were accustomed to a strong but complex system of their own, which to the Europeans seemed idiosyncratic. Maori blood relationships had shades of interpretation that didn't fit neatly into European terminology. There were, for instance, adoptions, half-siblings and children being raised by grandparents. Quite aware of this, Maori often used the English word cousin to describe a relative who may in fact have been of far more complex relationship because it satisfied European expectations and prevented embarrassment or further questioning. In time, Europeans came to understand the practice and a Maori person's cousin was regarded amiably by Europeans just as some kind of relation, possibly by blood, possibly not.

Maori, usually one step ahead in anything verbal, quickly turned the tables by deliberately using the word in wildly improbable and eventually comic contexts. Cousin became shortened to cuzzie, and its use was widely popularised by famous comedian Billy T. James, who deliberately publicised the word by using it to describe almost anyone Maori, in a way that was totally inoffensive but somehow took the mickey out of the European system (which Maori in general saw as somewhat straitlaced and restrictive).

Cuzzie is often shortened to cuz and tends to mean anyone who has some sort of family connection, which is curiously similar to Shakespeare's use. It is also matched with bro, short for brother, which also has a more generous meaning in Maori than in English.

(See also **Bro**)

D

Q Dag

The word dag is used in two different ways in New Zealand and each has a separate ancestry. When it means a lump of dry dung hanging off the back end of a sheep, the word is believed to come from an old British word much the same as tag, a bit hanging off.

A dag, meaning a lively fellow, is a different word altogether, which has existed since the 17th century. An artful fellow was called a *degen*, which meant a kind of sword, so if you said that about a person it meant he was a knowing blade or involved in a daring challenge. Its modern meaning isn't much different: being a bit of a dag means being slightly daring and probably amusing as well.

To rattle your dags is related to the first meaning and simply means to move fast. It derives from the obvious fact that, when sheep run, their dags often do rattle.

The word crops up in two different parts of New Zealand folklore:

(1) The name Fred Dagg, the popular comical creation of actor John Clarke, who epitomised the city-dwellers' perception of New Zealand farmers, and

(2) Dagg Sound, in Fiordland, named after a genuine seaman, Captain Dagg, who sailed there in 1804, took 5000 sealskins away and left his name behind.

Q Dairy

Although the word dairy retains its normal meaning within New Zealand — that is concerning milk and products derived from milk — it has developed a subsidiary meaning when the word is

59

applied to a small shop licensed to sell mixed groceries, milk, eggs, dairy products and perishables during and after normal trading hours.

At one time these perishables were delivered to city households from a base which, because of its connection with dairy produce, was called a dairy. As such produce was able to be stocked in small shops, by the late 1930s the term dairy shifted over to the shops themselves — even though they sold much more than dairy products.

Earlier called a mixed grocery shop, sometimes a lolly shop and occasionally — after the British equivalent — a corner store, the term dairy shop, then just dairy, settled in as the usual name in New Zealand.

In the United States a similar shop is sometimes called a convenience store, and sometimes a drugstore, which announces that it sells drugs and liquor, two commodities the New Zealand dairy does not normally stock.

(See also **Chemist**)

Daylight saving

It's a misnomer, of course — no daylight is actually being saved; it's only a trick to get people get out of bed an hour earlier. The idea began in New Zealand in 1909, and by 1928 had gone into law, putting New Zealand half an hour ahead in summer. The annual change became permanent in 1946 so that New Zealand was 12 hours ahead of Britain all year.

In 1974 a new Time Act was passed in New Zealand so that clocks went forward for four summer months. Farmers didn't like it at all, phone calls to and from foreign places became a minefield and airline schedules had to be planned months ahead. (In some cases, if you were flying to a place that didn't have daylight saving, it was possible to arrive before you'd left.)

One complaint that surfaced later went into popular New Zealand folklore: a woman is reputed to have criticised the system because all the extra sunlight was fading her curtains.

Q Dead loss

With its meaning of finite, utter, absolute or definitely ended, the word dead is a popular intensifier. A dead loss is a project, idea or job in which the rewards in no way compensate for the amount of effort put in. The term can also be applied to a person whose aptitude for whatever they're supposed to be doing is in the negative range.

Q Dear

Besides dear's usual meanings of beloved, precious or appealing, New Zealand has retained one of the less common meanings — expensive. When an object, a shop or a service is described as very dear, this does not mean you're fond of it — it means that the price is high.

Q Décor

Used to describe the general style or ambience of a house or business premise, and the aesthetic items added to its basic structure, décor in this exact sense is not widely used elsewhere.

Q De facto

A man and woman living together as if they were married, but without being legally married, are described as being in a de facto relationship. The basis of the term is the legal distinction between *de jure* (in law) and *de facto* (in factual existence). The term started as an adjective — a de facto relationship — but has become a noun — she was his de facto. It's not a familiar term in many places outside New Zealand, where terms like common law wife might be used instead. And within New Zealand, de facto is gradually being replaced by the less harsh-sounding 'partner'.

Q Dingbats

It is an American description, thought to be formed by combining 'ding-dong' with 'bats in the belfry'. In some places its meaning is a rather cruel description of genuine mental illness, but in New Zealand dingbat tends to be a more user-friendly indication that someone is zany, amusing or crazy in a friendly, amusing way.

Q Dip out

Meaning to fail, to be unsuccessful, to lose or not to make the required grade, this expression is possibly of Australian origin (it appeared in print there in 1965) but has a 'high frequency of use' in New Zealand.

Q The Ditch

It is properly called the Tasman Sea, but New Zealanders seldom refer to it by that name and Australians do so even less. (Australians have been known to refer to their 'Pacific beaches', as if the Tasman Sea didn't exist at all, when a great deal of Australia's east coast is entirely on the Tasman Sea.)

New Zealanders have been referring to Australia as 'across the ditch' since the early 1900s. It's a cosy way of pretending the distance between the two countries isn't very far: a ditch, after all, can be crossed with a jump. The 'jump' in this case is approximately 2000 kilometres — three hours by jet. England and France are separated by a much narrower stretch of water but nobody would dare call the English Channel a ditch.

A former Premier of New Zealand, Richard Seddon, speaking in pre-metric days, once said, 'There are twelve hundred reasons why New Zealand will not join with Australia — one for every mile between them.'

Dob in

To dob is an old British dialect expression meaning to put something down heavily. In Australasia the word gained a preposition and a slightly different meaning: to dob in came to indicate informing the authorities that someone was breaking the law. Variations arose: a dobber-in was the person who did the informing; sometimes he or she was just called a dobber.

As often happens with a vernacular expression, the term moved into more formal and official acceptance, even gaining a somewhat desirable connotation. In 2000, a city council campaign in New Zealand encouraged people to dob in vehicle-owners who were allowing too much pollution into the atmosphere.

 Docket

A piece of paper documenting a sale with information about items bought, price, delivery instructions etc., a docket often functions as receipt or proof of purchase. Commonly used in New Zealand, the word is unfamiliar in some other places — Americans, for instance, prefer to say cash ticket or cash receipt and are somewhat confused by docket.

(See also **Bill**)

Q **Dole, dole bludger**

'Dole' is related to the ancient Saxon word *del*, which described the piece of land given annually to peasant families to work. By 1911 there was not enough employment in Britain to go round and the British National Insurance Act allowed for 'a portion of financial help to be given to each man who could not find work'. Its correct name was unemployment benefit, but it gradually accrued the name dole — a more modern version of *del* in its ancient meaning of portion. *Del* also survives in the modern 'deal' — as in the portion of a deck of cards made available to each player.

Although the formal and official term for unemployment benefits is changed from time to time, New Zealanders still tend to refer to it as the dole. The term is not necessarily used in other countries where the same system might be called welfare, or relief.

A dole bludger is someone who bludges on the finance officially supplied by the government to people in need, without genuinely satisfying the eligibility criteria.

(See also **Bludge**)

 Dollar

When New Zealand discarded pounds, shillings and pence in 1967, and replaced them with a decimal system, the dollar became the basic unit of currency. This is not an American word, but originally Czechoslovakian. Dollar is derived from a place once called Joachimstal in Czechoslovakia (it is now called Jachymov), where there were silver mines. Coins from these mines were known as Joachimstaler during the 16th century, and eventually their name shortened just to *thaler*. That word travelled around Europe and surfaced in various languages as *taler*, *thaler* and *daler*, eventually becoming, in English, dollar.

 Domain

Normally this word means an area governed by a ruler or government, but in New Zealand domain can also mean a park — usually for public use and administered by a public authority.

(See also **Reserve**)

 Do your block

Since the 1600s, the word block has been used in English as slang for head, along with bun, loaf and nut. All of these are understood in Australia and New Zealand, but by the start of the 1900s, the locals were showing preference for block, especially in the term do your/his/her/my block, meaning to display anger in a definite and noisy way.

It is somewhat similar to being off one's block (though that is usually more panicky than angry), whereas to use one's block is to show good sense and reasoning.

Q Drapes

These are curtains — at least when they are made of solid woven fabric (not usually thin net-type window coverings). Developed originally as an upmarket term suggesting wide expanses of heavy damask in large mansions, drapes is now widely used for the most ordinary of fabric curtain drops.

Q Dressing gown

A loose-fitting indoors coat, usually without buttons but wraparound with a soft tie-belt, a dressing gown is worn for retaining modesty or body warmth or both, when one is not in a state of dress to be seen publicly. Or sometimes it is worn when just in the house, at leisure. The term is unknown to some visitors to New Zealand, who prefer the word bathrobe, or just robe.

Q Drongo

Not widely known outside New Zealand and Australia, the term drongo means a person who is very slow-witted. The drongo bird from Madagascar doesn't seem to be thought of as a stupid creature — rather the opposite, since it has a fierce reputation for protecting its young and will courageously attack much stronger predators. Nobody knows whether there is any connection between this bird and the popular use of the word drongo to mean an incompetent person.

There could have been some input from the fact that a racehorse of that name was prominent in Australia during the 1920s and, although a good galloper, always raced disappointingly.

Or maybe, just maybe, the New Zealand and Australian meaning arose simply because, whether the Madagascar bird is foolish or not, its name sounds funny. Stranger things have happened.

Q Drunk

In spite of European cultures' long association with alcohol and the recognition of what too much of it can do to a person, there still seems to be a faint sense of shame about actually saying the word drunk, with its 'low-life' connotation. It is used occasionally, but there is a tendency to substitute other words, such as squiffy, lit, shickered, merry, three sheets in wind, oiled, lubricated, pissed, sozzled, boozed, legless, full as a bull, off one's face, lashed, ripped, paralytic, sloshed, trollied, munted, full as a tick, plastered, wasted, tanked or fonged.

In the United States the word drunk is seldom heard at all. Writer Bill Bryson estimates that, by the mid-18th century, there were already over 200 words that Americans would say instead of drunk. They're still cautions about it: if forced into an admission that someone is drunk, an American will probably say inebriated or intoxicated.

Q Dummy

Although New Zealanders use dummy in many of its conventional contexts (e.g. for a ventriloquist's doll), the word also describes the rubber teat sucked on by babies. In other places this is often known as a pacifier, which has a certain logic to it. But so, too, does dummy, since one of the word's strongest meanings is an imitation of the real thing.

Q Dunger

This is a popular word for an old piece of machinery, usually a car. The dunger may be still effective, not even feeble, but it should be noisy. Dunger is believed to have developed from the sound of a less-than-perfect engine: dung-a-dung-a-dung.

Q Dunny

One of the many alternative terms for a lavatory, dunny's ancestor may be an old Scots dialect word *dunnakin*, which originally meant a kind of cellar. But there is strong belief that dunny, in New Zealand and Australia, has developed separately, based on the facility's close and inevitable association with dung.

(See also **Long drop**)

Q Dux

From the Latin for leader (which also developed into duke) the title dux is often given to the top academic student for the year in a New Zealand school. The United States has a valedictorian.

E

Q Easy as pie

This is a curious expression, since making a pie isn't all that easy. The saying seems to have surfaced about 1920 and there are two theories about its origin:

(1) There is an old alphabet mnemonic starting 'a is for apple-pie; b is for . . .' etc. Once a small child had mastered this, doubtless it would seem easy. Hence it is possible that the expression *easy as pie* developed from the children's alphabet rhyme.

(2) Another theory is that this is a rare example of bilingualism, *pai* being the Maori word for good, agreeable. So saying something was easy *and* pai indicated that doing it was not difficult, and was also pleasurable.

This explanation is doubtful but not impossible, although combinations of Maori and English are very rare.

(See also **Kapai** and **Half-pie**.)

Q EFTPOS

A minor revolution in cash commerce began in 1979 when computer technology made it possible for people to push a 'smart card' into a slot and, after punching in a PIN (personal information number), to receive cash in return (providing there was enough money in the account).

Five years later, in 1984, the system began to expand into retail outlets. A Shell service station allowed customers to pay by using their debit card (as opposed to a credit card), which magically transferred the requisite funds from the customer's bank account into the service station's account.

This system expanded into a vast network of retail outlets, and eventually 90 per cent of cash registers in New Zealand sprouted a hand-held device for tapping in your bank card PIN number and paying for items by instantaneously transferring that amount from your bank account into the shop's bank account. Besides being convenient for customers, the system suited retailers. Unlike a cheque, which required verifying and involved a wait for the actual funds to arrive, the new process ensured immediately that the customer's bank account contained the money being spent. The system was called electronic funds transfer at point of sale, which became EFTPOS, a word in itself. And New Zealanders are very keen on EFTPOS. By the end of 1999, EFTPOS terminals in New Zealand were processing 34 million transactions per month.

 Eh

A grammarian would call it a speech particle, but New Zealanders regard it as a speech essential. They add it to the end of a sentence to make it into a question: 'The bus leaves at six o'clock, eh?' Or sometimes it is added to a statement, indicating that the person being spoken to is expected to agree: 'This is a beautiful yacht, eh?'

Eh can also mean 'I beg your pardon? What was that you said?' Or it can express astonishment, indicating that you can't have heard properly: 'I've just won six million dollars.' 'Eh?'

The word achieved respectability in 1995 when a touring exhibition of New Zealand folk art had the formal title, 'Not Bad Eh!'

Eketahuna

Eketahuna is a perfectly respectable and pleasant township in the Wairarapa district, on the main highway between Masterton and Woodville. The place makes no claim to any sort of fame, but has had a minor sort of fame thrust upon it, because of its odd-sounding name. During the 1970s, journalist Gordon McLauchlan purveyed a frequent fantasy that Eketahuna didn't really exist, like Brigadoon. You never met *anybody*, he said, who had been to, or came from, Eketahuna. Although there's an element of comic plausibility in this, the town's Maori name has remained, and if anyone gets wound up about it, then the problem is theirs; the locals pay no attention.

The Maori name means running aground on a sandbank, because canoes could not pass any further than this up the Makakahi River. In 1872 Scandinavian immigrants bestowed the name Mellan Skog on the town, meaning heart of a forest, but after a few years reverted to the original Maori name.

 Eksetera

Coming directly into English from Latin, et cetera means 'and other things' (thus obviating the need for saying 'and' in front of it: to say 'and etc.' is actually saying and *and* other things). It is abbreviated as etc. and is correctly pronounced as ett-sett-er-ah.

However, disregarding the origins and the clear positioning of the letters in the abbreviation, New Zealand has evolved its own version of the pronunciation. A natural reluctance to say open vowels (e) combined with another reluctance to use the tongue more than necessary, has turned et cetera into eksetera, thus more or less reversing the internal components of the original spelling. This curious 'transposition of sounds in dialect speech' is called metathesis.

(See also **Metathesis**)

 Electric jug, hot water jug

Almost every New Zealand household owns a metal or ceramic jug with an electric element inside, which boils water for such domestic requirements as making tea or coffee. In Britain it is commonly called an electric kettle, or just kettle, just as, in New Zealand, the device is often referred to as the jug.

It comes as a major surprise that, in most of the United States, the nation credited with popularising most domestic labour-saving devices, this appliance and its name are virtually unknown. In the smartest and most luxurious kitchens, Americans usually tend to boil water in a saucepan on the stove — except for those rich establishments where boiling water is permanently available from a special tap.

Some motels provide a mug plus a small immersion-heater intended for boiling water to make instant coffee, and also sometimes available (but rarely) is a little jug of heavy plastic with a built-in miniature element, known as a hot-pot. But mentioning New Zealand's staple electric jug or hot water jug may meet incomprehension.

Engaged

New Zealanders say the phone or the line is engaged when the call they're making can't be connected because the phone they're ringing is already being used. Many visitors are not familiar with this word, preferring busy.

En suite

French for in sequence or following, the term en suite has been grafted into the building industry and applied to bathrooms that lead straight out of a bedroom and are generally used only by the occupants of that room. Although en suites are not unique to New Zealand the term is completely unknown in many other countries. When American accommodation has something similar it is often called a half bath.

Q Entrée

Accepting the meaning of this French word as opening or introduction, New Zealand restaurants offer an entrée as the opening part of the meal — an appetiser, a starter, a small offering of something tasty to set the scene for the main course to follow. Curiously, some other cultures use the word entrée to refer to the main course itself.

Q Erewhon

Samuel Butler wasn't an author when he came to live in New Zealand in 1860 but he became a famous one after he'd left. After exploring the Canterbury high country, he bought 5000 acres of 'unclaimed' Crown land which became the nucleus of what he called Mesopotamia Station, where he lived and worked for four years. In 1863 versions of his letters back to England were edited into a book called *A First Year in Canterbury Settlement*.

In 1864 Butler sold Mesopotamia and returned to England, where he developed his writing skills and in 1872 published the novel *Erewhon*. The title was an anagram of the word nowhere and the story was a satirical version of 'man seeking Utopia' in which Butler expressed astringent views about the English attitudes to religion and science. A sequel, *Erewhon Revisited*, was published in 1901.

Owing much to his experiences in New Zealand, *Erewhon* established Samuel Butler as a famous writer — one of the best known ever to have lived in New Zealand.

Q Eyes out

This term, which arose in New Zealand and Australia in the mid-1800s, remains in use. It means proceeding at full tilt, with top energy, as strongly as possible.

F

Q Fair go

An honest deal, with equitable treatment, is a fair go. It can also be a statement of surprise or mild interrogation: 'Fair go? Do you really mean that?' Although related to the British expressions fair deal and fair do's, New Zealand's preferred version is actually derived from the game of two-up, where the call fair go indicates that the game is all set up and ready to start.

Q Feijoa

Its formal name is *Acca sellowiana* but until 1815 nobody is sure what the fruit was called, if anything. A German explorer who discovered it in Brazil in 1815 named it after a Brazilian botanist called Joam da Silva Feijo. It was introduced to Europe in 1890. The feijoa was introduced into New Zealand in 1908 and flourishes in northern parts of the country where it is prolific in home gardens. There are now six varieties available here, varying slightly in shape, skin texture and colour.

All feijoas are low in calories and high in fibre and are a good source of vitamin C, which is at its highest level when the fruit is ripe and just picked. It is difficult to judge when feijoas are ripe, since their outside colour remains exactly the same. You have to cut into them and look. Ripe flesh is translucent; unripe flesh is white-ish and opaque. Over-ripe flesh has a brown shade.

Curiously, the fruit has not made any major impact in Australia or the United States, where it is very rarely found.

Fiord

Originally spelt fjord, the word comes into English from the Old Norse word *fjörthr*, meaning a long narrow inlet of the sea between high steep cliffs. The word *fjörthr* is also the ancestor of the English word firth — a narrow inlet from the sea (not necessarily with cliffs). The Norwegian origin and spelling of firth explains why it is sometimes spelt frith, which is closer to the original.

Fiord featured in early geographic descriptions of New Zealand: the *New Zealand Government Handbook* of 1903 referred to West Otago as a 'country of fiords'. But generally, the term 'sounds' has replaced fiords throughout New Zealand. One use of the word remains in the name of the extensive tourist area within Southland known as Fiordland.

(See also **Sounds**)

First generation

Internationally, the term first generation usually means the first person or family *born in* a locality or nation. New Zealand's usage has a slightly different slant. In official contexts the term is not used at all and appears to have no legal standing. But there is an understanding, at official levels, that when immigrants to New Zealand take out New Zealand citizenship, they become first-generation New Zealanders at that point.

If they do not take citizenship and just retain the status of permanent residents, they are not first-generation New Zealanders. (Thus, when immigrants take out citizenship, their New Zealand-born children are *second*-generation New Zealanders!)

 Fit as a buck rat

Meaning ready for action and very healthy, this phrase is similar to 'fit as a fiddle' but with a rather more typically New Zealand physical slant.

Flaked out

Thought to be originally a term used at sea, when a person became unconscious because of being deeply asleep or drunk, the term grew into general acceptance in New Zealand and Australia as 'flakers' or 'flaked out', meaning much the same thing, though in a sympathetic rather than pejorative sense. Flakers is not much used now, but Kiwis commonly say flake out to describe falling asleep, dropping from exhaustion or fainting.

A similar word — flaky — does not appear to be related either etymologically or in meaning, since it generally refers to a person of notable unreliability and insubstantial character who nevertheless is awake.

Q Flat

Most applications of the word flat have something to do with horizontal — the word's primary meaning. Originally a residence known as a flat was a set of rooms within a larger building, functioning as a separate residence and with all the rooms on one level. Real houses, often being more grand, had staircases between several floors. Two developments occurred:

(1) the growth in popularity of the word apartment, especially in the United States and

(2) changing patterns of architecture that meant a flat often did have a staircase.

Nevertheless, in New Zealand the word flat remains, whether it has staircases or not. Other developments are flatting (the act of living in a flat), and flatters (people who live in flats).

(For Americans, a flat means only a punctured tyre — possibly because it has become horizontal!)

75

Q Flat stick, flat tack, flat to the boards

All these expressions are familiar in New Zealand and Australia but rare elsewhere. They are variations on the idea of travelling as fast as possible and making the maximum effort, and probably arose from the fact that, when a car accelerator is pushed hard, it is flat and parallel to the floor of the vehicle. There is also a possible connection with the pilot's use of a joystick when flying.

And another possible derivation comes from horseriding. When the whip is held upright it isn't being used, but when it's horizontal then the horse is being urged to go faster. Hence, flat stick.

Where tack fits in, nobody is sure, though it possibly has nothing to do with engines and accelerators but with the fact that a tack is flat when it's been hammered in as far as it will go, unlike other forms of nail that have a head.

Q Flax

In 1770, James Cook and Joseph Banks recorded that New Zealand grew a widely used plant they described as flax. This appeared to be a case of mistaken nomenclature which has remained ever since.

New Zealand flax bears little resemblance to what is called flax in Europe. The New Zealand plant could possibly more accurately be called hemp. European flax (*Linum usitatissimum*) is an entirely different kind of plant. Its very useful fibre (from which linen is made) comes not from the leaves but from its stalks and the plant likes sandy, well-drained loam. New Zealand flax which tends to grow in swamps, was officially named in 1772 as *Phormium tenax*, based on the Latin for strong baskets. The Maori word is *harakeke*.

In pre-European times, Maori people used the very durable flax fibres for wide varieties of string, lines, cordage, baskets, mats, fishing nets and garments. Such was their skill with the plant that a trade industry developed, with expertly dressed flax fibres being made into rigging ropes for sailing ships and used in general rope-making. By 1873 there were 300 New Zealand flax mills in operation. The industry waxed and waned according to world events (such as the American Civil War and the First World War, which boosted demand). But the decline of sailing ships and the invention of synthetic fibres caused production to decline.

But useful though it still is, New Zealand flax plays no part in the production of fine high-fashion linens which according to international label laws, must be made from fibres of *flax* — European flax, that is.

Fly cemeteries

A certain kind of popular New Zealand delicacy consists of two slim layers of pastry or cake with a mid-section of compressed dried-fruit mixture containing a large proportion of raisins and currants. The biscuits — formally known as fruit squares — are pleasant and very moreish. But the cooking process makes the fruit mixture a glossy black colour and gives it a slightly chewy, toffee-like texture.

Early in the 20th century, some bright spark in Britain observed that this central fruit layer resembled a collection of squashed dead flies and coined the phrase fly cemetry. The term quickly took off and has been a jocular but recognisable nomenclature for many decades. But, well known though the description is, New Zealand manufacturers still call them fruit squares.

Q FOB

The term, pronounced as just fob, is an abbreviation of fresh off the boat, meaning immigrants who have come to live in New Zealand. Curiously, the term is used only about immigrants from the Pacific Islanders, not those from other places.

Originally the expression was pejorative and said behind the backs of those to whom it referred. But in time the Islanders themselves adopted the phrase and came to use it about themselves and each other without rancour.

By 1988 the term FOB was in print and in 1995 a Samoan play

entitled *Fresh Off the Boat* was publicly performed. Early in 2000 a Pacific Island concert in Auckland was widely advertised as a Fob Funkshun and featured a Polynesian singing group called The Brownies (another term of somewhat doubtful politeness used to refer to Pacific Islanders, unless they say it about themselves).

Fobs has also undergone a minor development among those who say it, and sometimes comes out simply as freshies.

Footpath

To New Zealanders it seems self-evident: the path followed by one's feet (though usually in an urban context — if there is no asphalt or concrete it is usually just a path). In other places a footpath is customarily referred to as a pavement or a sidewalk.

Fortnight

The word fortnight seems straightforward enough: it comes from the Old English *feowertiene niht*, and means, fairly obviously, 14 nights. Modern-day usage has brought some slight variations: a fortnight now indicates two weeks — but referring usually to the days, whether 14 nights are actually involved or not. It might be two working weeks, totalling only 10 days, or with a weekend in the middle, a total of 12 nights.

In spite of the minor variations, using the word within New Zealand rarely results in any confusion. Confusion can, however, be guaranteed by saying fortnight to an American. The word is virtually unknown there, and needs explaining if ever it is (inadvertently) used. Americans hearing the word for the first time, often assume it means four nights, which can wreck some planning.

Q Fossick

This is an ancient Cornish dialect word meaning to search unsystematically. The popularity of gold-seeking during New Zealand's early colonial times brought the word into extensive use as optimistic diggers fossicked through everything in sight, even other people's abandoned diggings. After the gold era, the word remained simply as a description of anyone rummaging through something in an absent-minded way, or searching a fairly wide area in leisurely fashion.

Q Foyer

In New Zealand the open interior space at which people arrive into a hotel, theatre, business building, and where the reception desks, box office or lifts are located, is known as the foyer. In some countries this is called the entry or the lobby — and visitors to New Zealand may be puzled when they find the letter F rather than L as an option on their downward lift.

Q Friesians

Originating in the Friesland province of Holland, these distinctive black and white cattle are excellent milk producers and a common sight in New Zealand. Although in this country they continue to be called Friesians (officially they're Holstein-Friesians), a great deal of the rest of the world calls them Holsteins, or Friesian-Holsteins.

Q Fringe

A fringe is an edging with (deliberately) overhanging threads past the perimeter of the main object. Hair styled to leave one section hanging over the forehead is also called a fringe — at least in New Zealand. Other places call this bangs.

Q Full stop

As Britain does, New Zealand calls the punctuation mark that ends a sentence or an abbreviation a full stop. Elsewhere it is often called a period.

Q Funny as a fit

This is a frequently heard New Zealand equivalent of 'funny as a fight' (as heard in some cultures), although, logically speaking, neither is actually very funny.

G

Q Gallipoli

It is one of the most famous placenames in New Zealand's history, but curiously, no place exists with that name. Many different languages tend to take a placename and transform it into a 'localised' version of its true pronunciation, sometimes with no visible logic. The city of München, for instance, is called Munich by people speaking English, who also refer to Firenze as Florence and Wien as Vienna. It can come as a surprise to English-speakers visiting those places to discover that the name they've always used is not in fact the 'real' name of the place.

So it is with Gelebolu in Turkey. Somewhere, sometime, an English-speaking person who may have had difficulty pronouncing it, chose to recast the name and say it as Gallipoli. This caught on and now English-speakers customarily talk about Gallipoli, usually unaware that this is not the real name. A visit to Turkey and a look at the battlefields of the First World War brings the true answer: the place is called Gelebolu.

Q Galoot

Although established in English since the early 1800s and still quite freely used in New Zealand, the word galoot isn't heard commonly in other countries. It means an awkward, clumsy person, but its origin is mysterious. The only known suggestion is that it somehow derives from the Spanish *galeoto*, meaning galley slave.

Gang

The word is believed to have grown from an Old Norse word *gangra*, meaning a group going together in company. The group in question could be quite lively and harmless, as in the early 'Our Gang' movies, and the famous boy scout Gang shows. But in more recent times the groups going together in company have acquired a definite connotation of being together for disreputable and criminal purposes.

One of the latter (a group together for disreputable and criminal purposes) did once laconically point out that the Rotary Club was, in its way, also a gang — though the name Rotary does not somehow have the same ominous ring as Hell's Angels, Headhunters or Mongrel Mob.

A hint of respectability also remains in terms like gang nails, where a flat piece of metal has numerous protruding spikes that can all be hammered in at the same time, for instance over two pieces of timber intended to be joined. The group (of nail spikes) is going together in company.

 Gap your axe

Wouldn't that gap your axe — wouldn't that annoy you — seems to be an expression of New Zealand origin. If you accidentally hit the blade-edge of your axe against something unyielding it will cause a notch and thus ruin the tool's efficiency.

The term may have begun with woodsmen and foresters and has been known since at least the 1930s. It was also used in the shearing sheds ('Wouldn't that gap your shears?') and has extended to anybody anywhere in an irritating situation.

Q **Gawk**

Although not a word of strictly New Zealand origin, gawk seems to be used more frequently here than elsewhere. Believed to originate from the Danish word *gaukr* (related to gape), it can be heard in Yorkshire meaning left-handed, but in New Zealand retains its more standard meanings of (a) a stupid, clumsy person, or (b) to stare at in a fixed manner. There's an occasional interaction with gawp, also meaning a stupid stare.

 ## Gentle Annie

An old popular song by Stephen Foster carries the lines: 'When the springtime comes, gentle Annie, and the wildflowers are scattered o'er the plain.' That's believed to be the source of the popularity of the placename Gentle Annie within New Zealand — several hills and gorges, a bridge, a bay and a hill track all carry Gentle Annie's name.

There's a legend, too, that a quiet-mannered 19th-century New Zealand barmaid called Annie made an impact on the local miners, so that her presence also contributed to the high profile of the name.

Either way — Stephen Foster song or real barmaid — Annie reached well into 20th-century New Zealand as well. A popular restaurant and a pleasant country music group carry her name, and an electrical appliance manufacturer capitalised on the warm popularity of the name by naming one of the washing machines in their range the Gentle Annie.

 ## Get in behind

This command given to (usually rural) dogs to come to heel has broadened into a gentle and semi-humorous way of telling someone to behave properly. Get in behind can also mean that a person or group is going to support a proposal (get in behind it) and is sometimes used as an ejaculation of surprise or disbelief ('You've won a free trip to Sydney? Get in behind.')

Q Get the wind up

An old armed services expression from the First World War, this is still in use in New Zealand, meaning to become nervous or afraid.

Q Gib, gib-board, gibbed, gib-stopping

In 1932 a New Zealand patent was filed for Gibraltar Board, interior wall panels of plaster and fibre that were 'as solid as the Rock of Gibraltar'. The term very quickly went into general use, usually shortened to gib. It became two verbs: gibbing, which is to affix the panels all over a wall, and gib-stopping, which is to fill the narrow gaps between the panels with hand-applied plaster.

Q Gidday

Always seeking the informal and, if possible, an abbreviation, New Zealanders and Australians had quickly reduced the English greeting 'good day' to 'gidday' by the late 1800s. By 1919 it was in print as an informal greeting — usually reproducing dialogue in which identifiably working-class people said it to more polite characters who stuck to good day. By the end of the 20th century the term was used throughout the country, as an ordinary method of greeting among most people but still with a slightly jokey air among the educated. Sometimes it's printed just as g'day.

In 1999 a child immigrant to New Zealand was found to be named Gidai, which was a perfectly valid forename in her homeland of Ethiopia. Benign authorities smoothly defused possible future confusion and embarrassment for the child by re-registering her with her middle name first, and gently advising that this order would make her life in New Zealand much easier.

Q Give it heaps

Another example of ellipsis, where some operative words are simply left out of speech and the listener's mind puts them back in. To give it heaps means to make a mighty effort, to ensure generous energy, to praise unstintingly. The missing word is what you're giving it heaps *of*. The context always ensures that both the user and the listener know what's being described, be it fuel, fisticuffs, energetic work, blame, speed, scolding, etc. The expression has been in use since the early 1980s.

Q Giving me gyp

It has nothing to do with gypsies. When your bad tooth nags you or the council sends you another notice about paying your parking fine, they're giving you gyp. But to put the expression in its full original, they're giving you a gee-up, as in kick-starting a stubborn horse. Over many years, this has shortened itself to gyp, but still means an annoying little irritation.

Q Give way

New Zealand follows the British custom of using the words 'give way' when notifying drivers to allow oncoming traffic through first. Other countries sometimes use yield.

Q Glow-worm

Its real name is *Arachnocampa luminosa* and it is formally described as the larva of a fungus gnat (thus, not really a worm). Its English name is borrowed from a European version of another glowing organism (which isn't a worm either, but a beetle) and has been in use in New Zealand since the luminous creatures were first noticed by early settlers who then wrote about them in 1848.

The New Zealand glow-worm goes through three life stages — larva, pupa, adult — and all three glow. The young ones glow to attract nourishment and the adult ones glow in order to attract the opposite sex. And glow-worms are well-trained ecologists — they can switch their lights off when they're not needed.

When they're young, their food is little insects flying around dark caves. The glow-worm lowers a shining 'fishing line' from its body to attract these creatures. Once their prey gets trapped on the sticky line, the glow-worm hauls up the line and eats lunch. Each glow-worm can drop as many as 70 of these glowing fishing lines, each up to 50 centimetres long.

New Zealand's most famous glow-worms are found in the Waitomo Caves, near Otorohanga.

Q Go bush

Although by definition forest means a large area thick with growing trees and plants, 19th-century immigrants from Europe seem to have displayed reluctance to say forest or woods, when they saw the rampant growth of New Zealand's treed areas. So bush became the most commonly used word for a large area thick with growing trees and plants.

In New Zealand, by 1810, the early English expression 'take to the woods', meaning either seeking refuge, or reverting to a simpler self-sufficient lifestyle, was replaced by 'take to the bush'. To go bush developed a slightly different meaning: it meant either to eschew urban life altogether and live by choice in a rural area without the usual attributes of comfortable living, or to hide deliberately, as from authorities such as the police. (Curiously this latter meaning need not necessarily indicate an actual forest: a person can be said to go bush while still remaining in a big city — but unable to be found.)

(See also **Bush**)

Godzone

This is short for God's own country, meaning New Zealand, a phrase coined by Thomas Bracken in 1890.

Bracken's words were:

> Give me, give me God's own country
> There to live and there to die
> God's own country, fairest region
> Nestling 'neath the Southern sky.

New Zealand Premier Richard Seddon boosted the phrase's popularity in 1906, after attending a conference in Australia. He sent a telegram home announcing that he was returning to God's own country. Seddon died the next day, but the phrase lingered on. It went through a slight semantic transformation when eminent poet Allen Curnow joined up the words and (slightly ironically) created a new word, Godzone, meaning New Zealand as a whole.

Some scholars believe that troops fighting in the American War of Independence used exactly the same expression in 1865, more than 20 years ahead of Thomas Bracken.

 Going nuts

Nuts has a long history as a slang word for insane, and New Zealanders occasionally use the term that way. But going nuts can also mean being angry, or being under such stress that insanity might result.

 Good as gold

This phrase has been used in England since the 1600s but there it customarily referred only to the manners and behaviour of a child. New Zealand has taken up the expression and made it into a wider affirmation — that things are going well, goodwill and approval are being expressed, everything is agreed and will proceed. (The late Dame Ngaio Marsh enjoyed it when she gave her weekly order to the butcher over the phone and he always replied, 'Good as gold.')

 ## Good on you, good for you

The phrase 'good for you' can be found in *Punch* around the turn of the 20th century. It seems to have faded from general use in Britain (supplanted perhaps by well done), but in New Zealand and Australia both forms — good on you and good for you — are commonly used.

 ## Goolies

Among the many terms for sex organs, goolies has crept into New Zealand from Britain as a semi-jocular name for testicles. It comes from the Hindustani word *goli*, meaning little round things such as a bullet, ball or pill.

 ## Gone to the pack

Closely related to the expression 'gone to the dogs', this probably puts out a similar canine image, in that gone to the pack means losing the leading position and becoming just one of the crowd. The expression refers to anyone who showed some potential but has gradually slipped to a mundane and lower level of life — gone to pieces.

 ## Go-to-whoa

Traditionally, whoa is the sound called out to cause a horse to stop. It is based simply on the ancient call ho, to attract a person's attention, apparently modified for horses.

The term whoa is widely used in New Zealand, though generally pronounced as 'woo'.

The phrase (from) go to whoa, meaning from start to stop, or from beginning to end, has been a familiar expression in New Zealand since the 1950s.

Also common is hearing the phrase in reverse, whoa-to-go, often used by car enthusiasts to describe how long it takes for a vehicle to get up to full speed from being stationary.

 Governor-general

Since signing a treaty with Queen Victoria, the country known as New Zealand (which had previously been a territory of New South Wales) became a colony and went upwards through several stages of national status (see **Kingdom**). Throughout all these changes, the sovereign remained Head of State, represented in the country by a resident dignitary of varying title: Lieutenant Governor, then Governor, then Governor-in-chief, then Governor of New Zealand and, from 1917 onwards, Governor-General.

The office is called vice-regal (standing in for the sovereign) and its bearer is addressed as Your Excellency. The main function of a Governor-General, as the highest-placed citizen in the land, appears to be ritual, but a Governor-General actually does more than that, since the pyramid structure of New Zealand's society is topped by a sovereign who doesn't live here. The Governor-General acts as Commander-in-Chief of the armed forces and participates in the formal rituals that keep a government running, accepting the writs that dissolve a Parliament before an election, then requesting the majority winning party to form a new government. The appointing of judges and receiving the credentials of ambassadors, top-level military matters and other factors that ensure the nation's smooth functioning, all require the signature of the sovereign or the sovereign's accredited representative. Parliament passes bills, but they do not become Acts (i.e. the law of the land) until signed by the sovereign's representative.

There is also a community role, whereby people feel the need of a head of state figure to lend stature to an event and will send invitations, numbering several hundred a year, asking the governor-general to attend. (In just one year Dame Catherine Tizard attended over 500 such community functions.)

 Greenstone

New Zealand is remarkably short of native animals, coloured native flowers and precious or semi-precious stones. One of the latter is greenstone, also known as New Zealand jade, which comes in two varieties: nephrite and bowenite (which in strict lapidary terms is not actually jade).

Besides being several beautiful shades of green, and thus attractive for body ornaments, the stone is also hard and durable and has been used for adzes, chisels and fighting clubs.

Initially in English it was described simply as green stone (1769) but had become hyphenated by 1817 into green-stone. The single word greenstone made its debut in 1864. The Maori language has been quite unaffected by this development and has called it pounamu all along.

 Grill

New Zealand tends to stick to the British use of grill, meaning food cooked one side at a time, by direct heat coming from above onto whichever side is placed upwards. All New Zealand stoves and cookers have a grill section that directs heat downwards for the purpose of grilling.

Americans prefer the word broil for the same process, broil meaning direct heat from above (not to be confused with boil). In the United States, food cooked on a barbecue, with the heat coming from underneath, is called a grill.

Q Grocer

Grocer comes from the old French word *gross*, meaning large amounts. In English, the grocer came to mean a dealer in foodstuffs and household supplies and his shop was called a grocery.

The word has all but vanished from the New Zealand vocabulary now. Since 1958, when the first supermarket opened in New Zealand, the supplies the grocer once stocked have been scattered through various supermarket aisles. Once supermarkets had a groceries section, which was later gentrified into baking needs.

Q Grotty

Grotty is derived from grotesque, meaning distorted and bizarre. Although the shortened form — grotty — was in use in the 1950s, it became popular during the 1960s, when the Beatles used it frequently enough for the rest of the world to take notice. It began as referring to something newfangled but not very effective, then expanded its meaning to refer to anything disagreeable — the weather, an untidy premise, a person, an irritation. Television character Reginald Perrin popularised the noun, grot, meaning goods and gifts of absolutely no use or value.

(Grot has been heard in Navy context, as a slang term for the mess room, but it has no connection with grotty. The naval use is believed to have been an abbreviation of grotto.)

Q Ground floor

The logic of this New Zealand name for the ground-level floor of any multi-storey building tends to flummox some visitors from other countries, who use a different system. Kiwi logic says that the ground floor is on the ground, and the next floor up from there is called the first floor.

In other places a different logic applies: since the floor at ground level is an actual floor, then *that* is the first floor, the next one up is the second floor and so on.

Although it's not a serious matter, it can cause confusion when Americans press a lift button in New Zealand and find themselves stepping out into a level they didn't intend to visit — and vice versa with New Zealanders in the United States. Visitors to New Zealand often assume that G on the lift button-board means garage.

 ## Grundies, grunds

This affectionate term for men's underwear is thought to be derived from a rhyming with undies.

 ## Grunt

Grunt means power or strength, in the abstract or the particular: for a car, say, an individual's influence or even the amount of garlic in a dish. It's often combined with 'A ton of . . .'

 ## GST

Although New Zealand had long had a sales tax, a new version was introduced in 1986, formally called goods and services tax (sometimes informally called Gestapo tax). Roughly equivalent to British VAT, or value-added tax, the New Zealand version is often referred to orally by a shortened version of its initials — pronounced 'jist'.

 ## Gully

It comes from the Latin word *gula* meaning throat (which also survives in gullet) and in England means a small valley, sometimes spelt gulley. Captain Cook described gullies he saw in New Zealand in the 18th century, and when he used the word he was describing ravines eroded by water courses. In later years New Zealanders have widened its meaning to a small ravine, gorge, eroded watercourse or depression on a flat that is sometimes treed, sometimes not. The word is far more commonly used in New Zealand than elsewhere, in preference to rather smoother words such as dell or vale.

Gumboots

The Egyptian word *kemai* gave the Greek language *kommi*, which became the Latin *gummi* and eventually the English word *gum* — a sticky substance that dried on exposure to air.

One version of this substance is a form of rubber, from which soft boots were made, reaching almost to the knee. They can be found in various colours (Britain favours green) but the great New Zealand gumboot was always black — carbon added to the rubber makes it black but also adds to the rubber's durability.

Until 1941, all New Zealand gumboots were imported, but from that date until 1977 they were made locally. Then production shifted to Malaysia.

The common British word for them, wellingtons or wellies, never totally dislodged the word gumboots (or gummies) in New Zealand. A popular comic song from Britain, 'Where would you be without your wellies?', was reworded for New Zealand consumption, and most famously performed by Fred Dagg (John Clarke). It substituted gumboots so that it went: 'If it weren't for your gumboots, where would you be?'

 A gun

This use of the word may date back to an expression with military connections, a big gun being either a large weapon or an important person. There was also a well-known shooting contest called the Top Gun.

In either context, the word big seems to have gradually eroded away, since the effectiveness of any gun summons up an image of an effective or expert person who gets things done — which is what the word has come (informally) to mean.

By the end of the 19th century, the fastest shearer in a gang was called the gun and the slowest was the drummer. The description has extended now to apply to anybody who's good at anything. In the 1990s, the young cricketers of New Zealand's team were called the Young Guns.

'In the gun' is slightly different. A descendant of the British term that describes someone who's drunk, it now means being in trouble of any kind.

Q Gung-ho

New Zealand's approbation for Rewi Alley, who went to work in China in the 1920s, helped to heighten the country's awareness of Chinese expressions. *Kung ho* in Chinese means work together. General Carlson of the US Marines, who had served with the Chinese Eighth Route Army during 1937–39, borrowed the words to use as a slogan during the Second World War. A popular 1943 movie with that title helped to spread the expression, which has developed to mean wildly enthusiastic — sometimes with a connotation that the enthusiasm prefers to override any appreciation of serious difficulties.

Q Guy Fawkes

Although Mr Fawkes' relevance to New Zealand was very slight, for many decades his most famous adventure was celebrated enthusiastically each year on 5 November — albeit often misnamed as Guy Fox Day.

Fawkes was a Roman Catholic who had left England because of religious oppression. He was brought back by a rebel Catholic group and, with several others, plotted to blow up King James I, his ministers and Parliament Buildings on 5 November 1605. The explosion never happened — Fawkes was captured, tortured and executed.

For centuries thereafter legions of people throughout the world celebrated on 5 November with bonfires, effigies and references to Guy Fawkes — even though he never actually accomplished what he intended. To most of them (including New Zealanders) it wasn't clear whether they were supporting Fawkes, should his plot have blown up Parliament, supporting the government's oppression of Catholics or just grabbing an excuse for a good party.

Towards the 1990s, the increasing toll of injury and danger arising from fireworks caused severe restrictions to be placed on their sale within New Zealand, but bonfires and fireworks still attract New Zealand children, who line up to celebrate on 5 November, even if they are a bit vague about *what* they are celebrating.

Q Haddit

This is derived (fairly obviously) from 'I've had it', but with one or two modifications. Originally the object was specified before the 'it': 'Don't worry about dinner, I've had it.' Over time, the object disappeared and the 'it' came to signify one's level of exhaustion or exasperation, life in general or a lost chance.

Gradually had it became one word, haddit, and as such could be preceded by either have or am. Or sometimes it appears just as an adjective — a haddit car engine, meaning one that's ruined and beyond redemption.

The term is also often concluded by the words up to here, accompanied by a gesture towards the throat, indicating gorge-level. But so familiar has up to here become, that the hand gesture is often left out.

Q Haere mai

In Maori, it translates literally as come here, come to me (one occasionally hears it called out to a child or family pet, when food is ready). But in wider and more general use, it means welcome.

Q Haka

To translate the Maori word haka simply as war dance is not strictly accurate. More correctly, it should be called a shouting dance of strength or a men's posture dance.

The term shouting dance is an apt description for several kinds of Maori performance, in which rhythmic shouting (rather than actual singing) is combined with vigorous movement. A haka — which perfectly combines shouting and vigorous movement — can indeed advertise intentions of war, and historically often has. But other versions of haka (there are hundreds) can also form part of a welcome, an affirmation of loyalty, a gesture of farewell or a challenge to supremacy. In terms of contemporary sport, the last sentiment is the one most popularly seen. In genuine wars, against other nations, the Maori haka has definitely meant business, and could freeze the blood of any foe who heard it. But a different kind of haka will occur in welcoming a VIP or farewelling a beloved. The key words are strength and passion, according to the sentiment being expressed at the time.

(See also **Ka mate, Ka mate**)

 Half-pie

This common New Zealand expression is a rare linguistic combination: an English word married to a Maori word, each retaining their original meanings but combining to form a unity with a third meaning.

Half is obvious: not complete, divided into two. Pai is the Maori word whose closest approximation (in English) is good, fine, commendable. So, when the two are combined, it is clear (to a New Zealander) that something is not commendable or good or properly done — it is only halfway there.

Although both languages freely transliterate each from the other, there are very few examples of Maori and English elements actually combining. One other possibility in standard usage is the term Maoridom, which attaches the whole word Maori (meaning people) to the suffix -dom (meaning domain), thus creating Maoridom — the collection of peoples and lands which occupy Maori life and thought.

(See also **Kapai** and **Easy as pie**)

Q Hangi

Underground cooking can be found in various cultures. The Maori version in New Zealand involves digging a deep hole and lining its base with very hot (and heat-retaining) stones. Wrapped bundles of food are placed in the pit over the heated stones, the bundles are covered with mats and then the mats are covered with earth and the hole totally filled. The captured heat and steam renders the food deliciously cooked some hours later.

Since the trouble taken to prepare and implement a hangi supposes that a large number of people will be fed from it, the preparation and eventual opening of the hangi is usually a joyous and hospitable communal occasion.

Q Hang of a

This is a qualifier or intensifier, which increases and emphasises the main point being reported. The expression appears to have arisen within New Zealand and Australia as a genteel version of a more daring intensifier — a hell of a — passing through the middle way of 'a heck of a'.

A lot of traffic is not as much as a heck of a lot of traffic. The apple crop is clearly a lavish one if it is a hang of a crop of apples.

Q Hapu

The Maori word hapu has two meanings. Its wider and more general meaning is extended family: a person's parents and grandparents, the sisters and brothers of those grandparents, and the children and grandchildren of the aunts, uncles and great-aunts and great-uncles. Sometimes hapu can be used to refer to one's sub-tribe.

Pronounced in a slightly different way, hapu also means pregnant.

Q Hard case

In its homeland of Britain, the description hard case meant a tough fellow, very likely the leader of a criminal gang and known for his courage and lack of fear. The term was used in that way in New Zealand until the early years of the 20th century, when the meaning underwent an almost complete about-face.

By the time of the First World War, a hard case was no longer a criminal but an attractive daredevil, probably quick on the uptake, capable of giving amusement and shrewd without being dishonest. In New Zealand, hard case had become a complimentary term.

Nowadays to call someone a hard case means he or she is already popular — likeable, a good sport, entertaining, irrepressible, incorrigible and unconventional, a person who thinks outside the square.

(Note: Hard case is not to be confused with head case, which means a crazy and unbalanced person.)

Q Hard word

Meaning to put verbal pressure on, in order to achieve a desired result — usually financial or sexual — this expression is now used fairly universally, but is believed to have arisen in New Zealand and Australia during the early years of the 20th century.

Q Hard yakka

If you hear someone say they've just done some hard yakka in the garden, chances are it's an Australian saying it — or a Kiwi who's picked up the expression from across the ditch.

Yakka is an all-Australian word: it's an adaptation of an Aboriginal dialect word *yaga*, meaning work. The term was adopted by white immigrants to Australia as a kind of slang term, and has been in general use since the middle of the 19th century. Adding the English word hard only reinforces the point. The effort of putting in posts for a fence doesn't sound strong enough as just yakka: it's hard yakka.

Head sherang

This description of the boss comes from the Urdu word *serang*, meaning the principal authority, especially the commander of a ship. The word somehow floated into English usage, meaning the absolute boss, the chief executive officer. It can be pronounced with just an 's' sound at the beginning, but most New Zealanders say 'sh'.

The odd thing is that, in New Zealand, the expression normally puts the word head in front of sherang — which is a tautology, like saying rich millionaire, because the sherang *is* already the boss.

Health

Although the word health normally indicates that a body is functioning well, in New Zealand it's often used to mean sickness. In spite of their titles, the Ministry of Health, health insurance, health professionals, health clinics and health legislation are entirely concerned with problems related to illness. Television and radio have health reporters who report on various matters to do with ill health. According to social commentator Richard Wolfe, this is called an inverted euphemism.

The word health is probably an optimistic gesture towards what people *want* to be (i.e. healthy) but the fact remains that, during their working day, health professionals only ever meet people who are ill.

For a while there was a moderate attempt to substitute the word wellness as a sort of middle ground, but the word never took off.

Herringbone shed

New Zealand farmers moved away from cowsheds in which the animals were milked in bails facing a wall towards a new design in which the bails were arranged in two angled rows that faced in opposite directions.

It took only one person to remark that, viewed from above, the new cowshed plan looked like the backbone of a herring — and the name stuck. By 1959 in rural circles, herringbone had become the accepted terminology.

 Hiding

Although this informal word for a thrashing is not a New Zealand development, it's not commonly heard elsewhere. Probably based on an old English reference to a person's being beaten on their hide, the expression's use in New Zealand has broadened to include many metaphorical situations where no body contact is involved, e.g. tennis matches or netball or even bridge games, where the loser can be said to have been given a hiding.

The expression is also frequently qualified by being elevated to a good hiding — a seeming contradiction in terms, though the 'good' in this case is simply a verbal intensifier and not intended to indicate moral worth.

 Hiding to nothing

This means bound to fail, a lot of effort being put into a project that is almost certain to fail. For instance, a sports team facing a match it knows it can't win, might say to each other 'we're on a hiding to nothing' before the game even starts.

Q Hissy fit

Undoubtedly based on the image of two cantankerous cats, and not provably of New Zealand origin, the expression is widely used here. It's not just a reference to an argument between people or a solo explosion of unease. Hissy fit has a connotation of suggested ridicule, as if a fuss is being made over an issue that doesn't deserve such energy.

Q Hogget

Hogget has a complex history and various uses. Originally a British word, it was used to describe a boar in his second year and there are still places that use the word when describing a year-old colt.

But in New Zealand hogget has moved firmly onto sheep and stayed there. The word is generally used to describe a young sheep when it loses its two centre front milk teeth (and therefore stops being a lamb) at approximately one year old. From then on (but only for the next 12 months), it is referred to as a two-tooth or hogget.

In terms of sheep meat, the youngest variety is lamb (up to approximately one year old), followed by hogget (the meat is never referred to as two-tooth, only the animal itself) and from then on mutton.

Q Hokey-pokey

Hokey-pokey ice cream, which characteristically used to contain irregular shreds of honeycomb created from breaking brittle sheets of confectionery with hammers, was first sold in New Zealand during the 1940s. It became so popular that marketing was increased, and 10 years later hokey-pokey ice cream was almost part of the New Zealand dietary landscape.

The word hokey-pokey is of very mysterious origin and nobody is at all sure how the expression arose. In New Zealand ice cream, it refers to scattered pieces of caramelised sugar with little bubbles created by the addition of soda. In other countries, a very similar confection is called honeycomb, humbug, butter brittle or seafoam candy, though none of these is exactly like the New Zealand version. (The United States has a similar ice cream called Rocky Road, but this contains lumps of stiff toffee rather than aerated crunchy honeycomb.)

In the 21st century, New Zealand hokey-pokey ice cream contains little rounded pellets rather than jagged shards. At the peak of the ice cream's popularity, New Zealanders ate 5 million litres of it per year.

 **Holiday**

Originally it meant a holy day and many cultures still use the term in exactly that meaning — one special day where something religious is commemorated. But in New Zealand the word is much more flexible, ranging from just one day (like Anzac Day) to a group of days centred around one special commemoration. A weekend in Rotorua, the annual three weeks away from your job at Christmas, or a full six-month cruise after you reach retirement age can all be referred to as a holiday.

Americans particularly are confused by this. For anything longer than one day, they go on vacation, based on the French word and first used in American English in 1878.

 Hongi

There is enormous variation in the body language of the greetings used by different cultures, from the Muslim salaam with hand to forehead through the complex protocol of Japanese bowing and the simpler European handshake (originating in a demonstration that no weapon was being carried in the right hand).

Maori have long held that the breath of a person's body is not only vital to the person concerned, but the action of sharing it with someone is a form of peaceful acknowledgement. Hence the traditional hongi, where noses are pressed together and the position momentarily held (usually twice), in order to share breath and thus the life force. The lips do not touch.

The hongi is a unique experience for visitors to New Zealand. A discreet explanation beforehand is usually offered.

 Hoo-ha

It sounds as if it could be derived from a Maori word, but it isn't. Hoo-ha is a nonsense word meaning commotion or fuss.

 Hooker

In some countries hooker can mean a prostitute, so the word must be used with caution in New Zealand, where hooker is spoken of very frequently — but to describe a player in the front row of a rugby scrum.

There was once a confusing incident when the wife of an American VIP stood next to a young professional sportsman at a New Zealand embassy party and, thinking he was placed somewhere in the diplomatic service, asked what his position was. He replied, 'I'm a hooker', and her somewhat flustered response was, 'Not tonight, thank you'.

 Hoon

The word's actual origin is unknown, but it has gone through distinct changes of meaning. Before the Second World War a hoon was a loutish exhibitionist, much as he is today. (Hoons always seem to be male.) But during the war the word underwent a complete reversal of meaning: thoughtful people who were conscientious objectors on other than religious grounds were known to the military as hoons (the others were called religoes).

After 1945 the word remained in use, but reverted to its earlier sense and a hoon once again became a stupid person, a lout, an exhibitionist.

A few grammatical extensions also exist: hoonish, hoonism, hooning, hoondom, hoon around, hoon it up, a bit of a hoon, hoon-chaser (traffic police) and hoon-bin (place where drunken football louts are put to cool off). Medicos attending emergencies involving reckless young males use the word hoon to stand for 'has only one neuron'.

A comedy character in a New Zealand television series somehow placed himself perfectly in viewers' minds simply by being named Darryl Hoon. And an Auckland wind instrument music group called themselves the Newton Hoons, presumably a nice word play on the fact that they played horns.

Hooray

For some unknown reason, New Zealanders have developed a resistance to saying hurrah, which is a common enough exclamation in Britain. To Kiwis, hurrah seems reminiscent of upper-class twits, and the word is seldom if ever heard here.

The New Zealand hooray is simply a variant on the British hurrah but, besides being different in pronunciation, it has also developed an extra meaning: an informal version of goodbye. (This confuses some British people coming to New Zealand who, when bid hooray, think they are being commended for something.)

A vague belief that hooray is an Anglicised version of the Maori phrase haere ra is entirely without foundation.

Hori

Maori personal nomenclature was organised on a different system before Europeans arrived in New Zealand. But in a very short time Maori (always very much attuned to interesting verbal effects) became intrigued with the names of their white neighbours, and in many cases honoured those they thought honourable by simply taking on their names — as in Maori families now dating back over 100 years called Nathan or Williams.

Often, the adopted names were smoothed out into a mellifluous Maori version of the original — as with the name Henare (Henry) or famous chief Tamati Waka Nene, whose Polynesian-sounding name is actually Thomas Walker, revisited.

The name George appeared to have a particular fascination. Transliterated into a language with no g it came out as Hori — and stuck. Hori/George became such a frequent and familiar name for Maori men, that during the 19th century the word was frequently used to designate any Maori at all whose actual name one didn't know. He became, in casual speech (offensively) just Hori, or *a* hori. It is not acceptable usage now.

 ## Hosed off

It means that someone is very displeased. The expression has been in use since at least the 1950s and writer David McGill reports that it is possibly related to a 16th-century English expression of disbelief 'in my other hose', where hose means stockings.

A more general supposition is that the term is a simple explanation of how anyone would feel if a fully active hose of water were turned full upon them. Equally common in New Zealand is the saltier pissed off, which may have been replaced by hosed off in polite company.

 ## Housie

Sometimes given its full title, housie-housie, this is a term describing a game similar to bingo.

Q How are you?

This is the most-asked rhetorical and ritual question in New Zealand. A real answer is not expected, just the return ritual, 'Fine, thanks'. Sometimes even that reply is bypassed and you will hear a radio interviewer say, 'Good morning, how are you and when did the news reach you about the shipwreck . . .'

Outside certain particular contexts, such as a hospital room, it's not done to voice any genuine concerns about health. Indeed, it's a kind of New Zealand joke to say of someone, 'If you ask her how she is, she tells you!' Other societies manage to express hope that a person is in good health without actually asking them: the Maori kia ora, for instance, and the old English hail (which originally meant I hope you are healthy and whole).

Q Hui

In simple terms, hui is a Maori word for a meeting, but not just a casual get-together or a purely social occasion. A hui is a meeting with a purpose, usually to discuss a project, policy, business tactic or a religious matter. It can also be a big reunion of family members or a gathering to celebrate an ariki (chief or aristocrat). Thus a hui is better described in English as an assembly.

A hui is usually held on a marae, where tradition demands certain behaviour and formalities and speeches that follow a ritual pattern. Depending on the purpose of the hui, the speeches may become quite heated, but even so, proprieties are observed.

Mostly, a hui is an all-Maori affair, to discuss or celebrate matters concerning only Maori people. But there are times when both Maori and non-Maori opinions are required: if it is decided to examine the matter 'in the Maori way' then a hui will be held, attended by Maori and non-Maori, and Maori protocols will prevail.

I

Q 'I can do it in . . .'

This is the usual response to the question 'How far is X?' The reply estimates the driving time required to get to X. Because fast efficient driving is often equated with machismo and supreme control, it's normally wise to regard the given time as one which greatly exaggerates the average driving speed.

Q -ish

It is related to the German suffix *-isch*, from the Greek *–iskos*, meaning approximately. This qualification is extensively used in New Zealand, exactly as intended. Widely and universally understood, it is a kind of shorthand way of saying maybe, possibly, I'll know later, I'm guessing. If you ask someone if they will call next Saturday and they say 'Yes, sevenish', they're giving an approximate time only.

Q Iwi

In Maori, the word iwi indicates all those to whom one is related by blood. Another word that covers this is tribe, but a more familiar word in English terms is kin, people to whom you are related by blood.

J

Q Jack-up

Thought to have evolved among New Zealand troops during the Second World War (connected with raising a vehicle with a jack), jack-up has little connection with its similar-sounding British cousin. A New Zealand jack-up has two distinct shades:

(1) To fix up, cause something effective to happen or make a quite respectable arrangement — 'Mary jacked up an appointment for me with her boss' or 'I jacked up a temporary bank loan'.

(2) To wangle, contrive, engineer something to happen, usually to your own advantage — 'He jacked up the tickets so that the girl he fancied had to sit next to him'.

Q Jam

Whole fruits, when chopped and boiled in sugar, become a firm mixture that sets into a near-solid state and lasts for a long time before decaying. The name jam is believed to have arisen (in the 18th century) to describe this delicacy because of the basic necessity that the fruit be cut or squeezed and damaged as a preliminary to the cooking process.

Except for marmalade, New Zealanders use the word jam freely to describe the result of the cut-fruit-squeeze-and-cook-with-sugar process. But the word is sometimes not used in other places. British people often speak of preserves and Americans call it jelly. (The latter can cause confusion: a Chinese translator, influenced by American speech, once described a crowd of cars brought to a standstill as a traffic jelly.)

Q Jandals

In 1957 a New Zealand businessman, Anthony Yock, went on a trip to Japan and took an interest in the Japanese sandal known there as a *geta*. It has a sole (sometimes wooden) and an ingenious strap that passes around the big toe. Mr Yock wondered if, made in rubber, it would work just as well.

He organised a version to be made in a New Zealand garage and judiciously registered the trade name jandal (short for Japanese sandal). The result was immediate. Before long it seemed that every New Zealander owned at least one pair of jandals — and was calling them by that name.

But imitators discovered that, legally, they had to use a different name, so other firms and other places now call them something else — flip-flops, floppies, thongs (some places in the United States call them slippers and to the French they are known as Le Slap). But in New Zealand the word jandal has become part of the language.

Q Janola

Although it is the brand name of a specific New Zealand product, in common conversation Janola has come to mean just bleach — any kind of bleach. This could be partly because the name of this particular bleach liquid somehow *sounds* very antiseptic and effective. But this was not planned so: Kiwiana researchers Stephen Barnett and Richard Wolfe reveal that Janola was named in honour of the New Zealand bleach originators' wives — Jan and Nola.

(Some years later the familiarity of the brand had a slightly unfortunate backlash for a young woman who insisted her work colleagues called her by her full hyphenated forename, which was June-Ella. The colleagues, considering this rather pretentious, of course dubbed her Janola.)

Q Joe

In New Zealand this word is frequently used to mean a condom, which can be referred to as a joe or a joey. Other substitute words for the same item (a johnny, a raincoat) fulfil the same function. But the word joe is to be treated with care, because in various countries it means entirely different things. In Australia a joey is a baby kangaroo, tucked in its mother's pouch. Or sometimes an Australian will use it to mean a lie or a fake.

Scottish dialect has the word yowe, meaning an adult female sheep (i.e. ewe) which occurs in the Australian song 'Click Go the Shears' ('curses the old swagger with the bare-bellied yowe') but unfamiliarity with the old dialect word in contemporary Australia has seen yowe in that song become transmuted into 'a bare-bellied joe', thus adding one more application.

In the United States a joe can mean just an ordinary man, or, curiously, a cup of coffee (named for Josephus Danish, who as Secretary of the US Navy in 1913, banned alcoholic drinks from naval ships and would allow only coffee). There was also a period when a baggy pullover was called a sloppy joe. In Britain a joe can sometimes mean a small silver coin, or a kind of canal boat.

Only New Zealanders seemed to have made poor joe slightly scurrilous.

Q Jokers

Apart from meaning someone who plays tricks, the word joker is close in meaning to others indicating an ordinary man — a bloke, a guy. It dates back to a British slang word meaning both a jolly fellow (a joker) and an ordinary chap. Samuel Pepys uses it that way in 1669, writing that he had lunch with some old jokers — exactly as the word would be used in Australasia.

Since the 19th century it has been used in Australia and New Zealand far more than in most other places. Sometimes it can be transferred to other living creatures — 'the puppy was a friendly little joker'.

Q Judder bars

Upraised ridges across a roadway, whose presence persuades motorists to slow down before crossing them (if they value their car roof, their false teeth, their fragile parcels and their children's heads), judder bars are so named because of the sensation caused by driving over them too fast. They are known elsewhere as speed bumps.

K

Q Kai

This Maori word for food is quite often heard with a qualifying word to designate a certain kind of food, e.g. kai moana: food from the sea.

Q Ka mate, Ka mate

Of thousands of Maori haka, this one is probably the most famous among non-Maori and is regularly performed by the All Blacks before test matches. It was composed around 1820 by the great Ngati Toa chief Te Rauparaha. At the time, he was involved in a bitter battle with another chief, and had taken temporary refuge in a neighbour's kumara pit. The neighbour was a hirsute man, whose wife crouched above the pit to hide the precious person hiding in it. To be beneath her was not a dignified situation for a high-ranking chief who, when he emerged from the pit, gave a passionate oration before going back into battle:

Ka mate! Ka mate!
Ka ora! Ka ora!
Tenei te tangata puhuruhuru
Nana nei i tiki mai
I whakawhiti te ra!
Upane! Upane!
Upane! Ka upane!
Whiti te ra!

Go away Death, bring Life,
There stands the hairy man who brought light to darkness
Take one upward step, one last upward step,
Then step forth — into the sun that shines!

One aspect about this haka which is seldom mentioned is that it is in waltz rhythm — very unusual for an energy-rousing war-like statement.

 Kapai

In strict translation it means 'that — good' (the Maori language has no verb 'to be') but in wider use kapai is a general term of approbation, meaning that everything is going smoothly: that's commendable, well done. The word is frequently used in an English-language context.

The opposite expression, kakino (that's bad), does not seem to have crossed over into English usage, and is seldom heard.

 Karakia

Although it comes close to the English word prayer, a Maori karakia has a slightly different dimension. Both a prayer and a karakia address words to an unseen presence and are framed to communicate with a greater power. But where a prayer can become a ritual event, even a daily practice, a karakia tends to be created anew for each occasion: it attempts to express the mysticism of a particular event or situation, rather than having a ritualised regular structure.

 Karanga

A chanting call in the Maori language, invariably performed by women, which signifies the beginning of an event or gathering.

Since many events of importance take place outdoors, a particularly incisive vocal tone is associated with the ritual, and only women who can command this compelling sound are invited to present the ritual chant.

The karanga, which may have a complex structure, includes information about the event that is about to occur, who will be present, whether they are to be welcomed or cautioned, and calls for unity among all involved.

Under normal circumstances one woman (usually of some seniority or importance) performs the karanga, but on special occasions it becomes a two-person call, and, at the highest level, three women alternate and combine.

Q Karitane

Karitane is the name of a tranquil Otago settlement just north of Dunedin. The word is subject to several interpretations — nobody is sure what the original Maori settlers may have intended by the name.

The place became well known because of Sir Frederic Truby King, who had a holiday home there in the late 19th and early 20th centuries when he was medical superintendent of Seacliff Lunatic Asylum. In the 1900s he turned his attention to the feeding and care of infants and in 1907 established the Society for the Promotion of the Health of Women and Children. This became known as the Plunket Society, after the New Zealand Governor's wife, Lady Victoria Plunket. According to the *Dictionary of New Zealand Biography*, Truby King took ill babies into his Karitane house, and thus the first of several Karitane hospitals was established. The word Karitane was also used to describe the nurses throughout New Zealand trained in child care.

(The word Karitane also survives in a less-welcome form: the colour of excrement from young animals, particularly calves, is often described as Karitane yellow.)

(See also **Plunket**)

Q Kaumatua

There is no simple English equivalent for this word, except perhaps sage, maybe mentor or, at a pinch, guru. A kaumatua is an elderly Maori man who has acquired dignity and good sense along with his accumulated years, and whose opinions and advice are taken seriously by younger people. The term is not a bestowed title; nor does it come automatically along with the grey hair. A certain overall charisma, a distinguished manner and bearing, combined with a track record of experience, somehow amalgamate so that other people begin to use the word kaumatua about a man — because he is both old and wise.

Q Kia ora

A Maori term of some versatility, which does not translate smoothly into English, kia ora is frequently perceived as a Maori form of hello, though this is not strictly accurate. The best way of understanding kia ora is to regard it as a hope for good health, in which case it stands closer to the English expression, hail.

The health or, better, the well-being implied in kia ora can also apply to concepts or projects — saying kia ora to someone about to embark on a journey, a new job or even a marriage, is akin to wishing that all good things will come to him or her.

Q Kindling

To kindle means to inflame. To be absolutely correct, you light a candle, because its main purpose is to give light, but you kindle a fire, because it is required for its heat.

Kindling or, more correctly, kindling wood, is the collection of thin wooden strips that initially catch light and then encourage a fire to burn. A general downturn in the number of fireplaces in New Zealand homes has rendered kindling a somewhat rare word, but it is still used, whereas in some countries the term is quite unknown.

Q Kingdom

Most New Zealanders, if asked to describe the constitutional status of their country, give a somewhat mumbled answer. Many confess they simply don't know. Even schools can be a bit vague about it. The answer is that New Zealand is a kingdom.

New Zealand started out as a legal territory (attached to New South Wales) and was transformed into a colony in 1840. Elevation to a dominion came in 1907.

A change came in 1953 when the Royal Titles Act resulted in Queen Elizabeth II becoming head of state specifically for New Zealand, and New Zealand itself became a sovereign independent realm — otherwise known as a kingdom.

(See also **Queen of New Zealand, The**)

Q King Country

The nation known as New Zealand was largely established under the reign of a female monarch, Queen Victoria, with references to her and her name cropping up all over the place. Why, then, is one area of New Zealand called the King Country?

The name is a legacy of the Maori King Movement established in the area in the mid-19th century, though this was subject to criticism from imperialists who thought the world began and ended with Victoria. In 1863 the second Maori King, Tawhiao, took refuge in the western central part of the North Island, and from then on the area was informally referred to as 'the King's territory'. Usage gradually abbreviated this to King Country, which became so usual that an 1884 government survey formally conferred King Country as the official name of the area. The Maori name for the region is Rohe Potae, or the rim of the hat.

Q Kiri

In most languages, including Maori, a name, especially a first name, doesn't necessarily have a meaning. But the Maori word Kiri does have several meanings: it refers to a covering or surface — and that can be something like the bark of a tree or the sweet top layer of a fruit. In some dialects the word can also represent the sound of a bell (though that meaning must have evolved during fairly recent history — Maori couldn't have heard the sound of a bell until early in the 19th century).

In 1944 when Tom and Nell Te Kanawa decided to call their new daughter Kiri, they were naming the baby after her grandfather since, like many Maori names, Kiri is not confined to either gender. They also unwittingly provided the child with a name whose faintly exotic sound was no hindrance to a future international career: it is easy to say in any language, ends with a vowel (particularly suitable for speakers of Japanese, Italian and all Latin languages) and has a musical sound all on its own.

As a journalist once enthused, 'Kiri — say it soft and it's almost like singing . . .'

Q Kiwi

When information first began to filter through to Europe about a very strange bird found in New Zealand, people developed an odd concept of what it looked like because early drawings were made by looking at the dried skins that had been sent back. And attempts to transliterate the Maori name came out as kee-vee or sometimes kivi-kivi. It's hard to know why it gained the name kiwi in Maori. If ever you hear one, or a recording thereof, the cry often doesn't sound anything like kiwi.

By 1887 the kiwi was being depicted in a university coat of arms, and by the start of the First World War, with a capital K, the term was widely used to describe New Zealand soldiers. It has grown since to become shorthand for sharemarket dollars, a furry fruit, a boot polish — and New Zealand citizens in general.

Q Kiwiana

A word immortalised by researchers Richard Wolfe and Stephen Barnett, whose various books on New Zealand's social history unearthed a tonne of nostalgia and uncovered surprising amounts of Kiwi ingenuity, advertising, customs, preferences and attitudes, all of which add to the background and heritage of any person known as a New Zealander. Kiwiana sums the situation up perfectly and is defined by the *Oxford Dictionary of New Zealand English* as 'items redolent of New Zealand life and culture'.

Q Kiwifruit

The fruit originated in the Yangtze Valley in China, with the Chinese name *yang tao*, usually translated as monkey peach. The fruit was available in New Zealand from 1914. For many decades New Zealanders knew it as Chinese gooseberry and it wasn't considered a big deal. New Zealand first exported the fruit to England in 1952 but when exports began to the United States (where it was unknown), there were problems: Americans were confused by the name gooseberry (when the fruit was nothing like any other kind of gooseberry).

An attempt to rename the fruit as melonettes struck disaster when it was realised that anything to do with melons attracted a high import duty. The Turner brothers, of the export firm Turners and Growers, knew that military servicemen overseas were universally known as Kiwis, so in 1959 the Turners decreed that, at least when dealing with the States, the Chinese gooseberry would be dubbed kiwifruit. The term won universal acceptance in a very short time.

(See also **Zespri**)

Q Knackered

This means to be exhausted, worn out, damaged or ruined. There are two significant applications of the word knacker, either a slang term for testicles, or a long-standing meaning for old horses with no further utilitarian value, and the yard where they are slaughtered. With these two influences, the term knackered arose among the armed services early in the 20th century. It is still in fairly common use throughout New Zealand (at least among men) but not so much elsewhere.

Q Knock off

Knock off means to finish, as in 'we knock off work at 6 p.m.', but it can also mean to sell, as in buying a new car and knocking off the old one at the weekend sale. In some circumstances the term can also refer to a job that has been definitely completed, e.g. the quote attributed to Sir Edmund Hillary, after climbing to the top of Mount Everest: 'We knocked the bastard off'.

Q Knock up

Although most New Zealanders are aware that this expression has an entirely different meaning in other places (i.e. becoming pregnant), it is still used throughout New Zealand in a totally separate way.

In the right context, to knock up means to visit without prior arrangement (usually very early or very late — the door-knocking wakes them up), either friends you already know, but who aren't expecting you right then, or strangers who happen to live close to where some emergency has happened.

It can also refer to deliberately setting up the knocking or visiting in advance, such as asking a motel office to knock you up at 6 a.m. It is not wise to put this request to anyone running a motel office in the United States.

In quite a different context, to knock up can also be to construct something in a hasty or temporary fashion, e.g. a shelter. This meaning is synonymous with knocked together.

 Koha

Maori for a gift, it can vary from something small and personal given to one person by another, to a quite large donation of either goods or money which, in some circumstances, can be recognised legally as a form of tax-free transaction. In general terms, the word koha immediately conveys the information that something advantageous or pleasant is to be bestowed, without any payment being required.

 Kohanga reo

Usually translated from Maori as language nest, the kohanga reo system began in 1982 to provide groups of pre-school Maori children with educational and cultural activities — taught entirely in the Maori language. Within 20 years there were over 600 kohanga reo groups throughout New Zealand.

 Koru

A scroll pattern spiral depicting a stylised version of an uncurling young fern, this characteristic shape appears in differing contexts throughout Maori history. Air New Zealand established a form of koru as their trademark, and the late Austrian artist and architect Friedensreich Hundertwasser, who lived in New Zealand, fought ardently for his koru design to become the official national flag.

Q Kuia

In Maori terms, a kuia is an elderly woman who is respected for her wisdom. The term is not automatically acquired simply by growing old, and it is not officially granted by any higher authority at a specific moment. To be a kuia is a state some women grow into gradually; as respect for them develops, so the word starts to be used about them.

Q Kumara

Sweet potatoes are found in other cultures. The most commonly used version in New Zealand, the kumara, was designated by food researcher Digby Law as not native to this country but brought in by whalers in the 1800s; its closest relatives appear to be South American. But besides taking over the name kumara from the root vegetable brought to New Zealand earlier by Maori, the locally grown kumara gradually developed a style of its own. The most recognised and used strain of the plant is *Ipomoea batatas*, a member of the convolvulus family (kumara are not related to potatoes).

Commercially grown in big quantities, the New Zealand kumara is a staple and welcome vegetable. The most popular type is large and plump, with a distinctly purple skin and gently gold flesh. It is much missed by expatriates who have access to other sweet potatoes, such as Portuguese and contemporary South American, which they declare are not the same. Maori will sometimes say they have heard news or gossip on the kumara vine.

(One of Digby Law's cheekiest culinary creations was a sweet-potato dish cooked with spice and orange peel, and named Kiri Te Kumara.)

L

Q Labour Day

It's an odd name for a holiday on which people look forward to leisure, rather than work! But the original intention was to celebrate the acceptance of an eight-hour working day as the norm in New Zealand. (The move towards that started in 1840.) A Labour Day holiday started in 1899, although the eight-hour day was actually not law at that point, and only tradesmen and labourers were allowed to celebrate with a day off. Early on, Labour Day fell on a Wednesday, but in 1910 it was reasoned that this wasn't a good idea, and Labour Day (now a much more general holiday) was shifted to the last Monday in October.

Q Ladies a plate

The ancient custom of combining fellowship with food resulted in this New Zealand expression which reflects the pragmatic view that hospitality shouldn't all be provided by one host. More economical than hiring a caterer, and normal practice in rural areas, 'ladies a plate' on an invitation meant that the women attending would each bring some appropriate self-prepared food. Sometimes the provision of a 'plate' freed the woman from paying any entrance fee, or she had the same option as the males — namely paying the entrance fee but *not* providing food.

The expression became widespread during the 1920s and remained in use through the rest of that century, though now it is seldom heard in urban areas, where variations of the contributing theme still occur under the guises of pot luck suppers and progressive dinners.

Q Lamington

This is a baked delicacy of sponge-cake, cut into cubes, coated with chocolate and then sprinkled with coconut. (A variation using pink icing instead of chocolate is known as raspberry lamingtons.) The confection is named after the popular Scottish aristocrat Lord Lamington, who was Governor of New South Wales in 1896.

Julia Robinson, author of *Voices of Queensland*, reports that the sporty Lord Lamington regarded the cakes as 'bloody woolly and poofy' but nevertheless the name lamington has been used for them ever since. Subsequent holders of the title Lord Lamington must have been subject to many irritating jokes about chocolate and coconut whenever they met an Australian or New Zealander. But it won't happen any more — the cakes remain, but the last of the Lords Lamington died in 1951.

Q Larrikin

A larrikin is a high-spirited young person, usually male, whose behaviour occasionally — but not always — verges on social irresponsibility. The term appears to originate in a very old British dialect word meaning a mischievous and frolicsome youth and could be one of those words which came with the 19th-century immigrants to the southern hemisphere, where its use continued while the word was dying out in Britain.

When the Duke of Edinburgh made a supposedly offensive remark to an Aboriginal in 2002, a British newspaper subsequently interviewed the man involved, who commented, 'We weren't offended — the Duke was just being a larrikin' — which the newspaper felt obliged to explain to British readers.

In New Zealand larrikin has given rise to the word larrikinism — activities carried out by larrikins. But there is a subtle difference: calling a young man a larrikin can sometimes be friendly and mildly indulgent, but what the larrikins do — larrikinism — often carries a connotation of censure.

Q Laughing gear

This term for a mouth was made popular by (and maybe also invented by) author Barry Crump in the 1960s.

Q Lay-by

This system allows a customer who cannot immediately find the full price of a retail item to pay a portion of the price, and so reserve the item on lay-by until full payment (usually in instalments) has been completed. The term has been used in New Zealand and Australia since the 1920s.

In some other places, the term lay-by has a completely different application: it means a pausing space for motorists at the side of a busy road.

Q League

A league is an association or union of people who work together; usually they're members of something. In that context, the word comes ultimately from the Latin *ligare*, meaning to bind. (It has nothing to do with the archaic measure league, as in the seven-league boots of fairytales, which comes from a different Celtic word that finished up being spelt the same.)

In 1895 some British rugby union clubs broke away from the Rugby Football Union and called their new version of the game Northern Union. But in 1922 the organisers decided to change the name to Rugby Football League.

The crucial point of difference seemed to be money. Some players couldn't afford to take time off work to play traditional rugby so the league people set up a financial structure. This was anathema to the Rugby Union officials who insisted on their game remaining amateur for many more years.

In time the name Rugby Football League was slimmed down to just league.

Q Lemon & Paeroa

By custom and usage, the two words describing this flavoured mineral water have been unified into the abbreviation: L&P. The little town of Paeroa, on the edge of the Hauraki Plains, was home to a spring of fine mineral water, which was visited and analysed by government balneologist Dr A.S. Wohlmann in 1904. Three years later, aerated cordial manufacturers Menzies & Co. mixed lemon juice with it, and a national icon was born (though in those days it was called Paeroa and Lemon). The trade name Lemon & Paeroa was registered in 1914.

Transporting the water to far-off bottling plants became expensive, but since Dr Wohlmann had analysed its contents so efficiently, and obligingly left the chemical formula of the water, Menzies were able to recreate an exact copy. So the sparkling sweet-bitter soft drink continues, now marketed as being 'world famous in New Zealand'.

Q Lifestyle

This word is now usually found as part of the term 'lifestyle block', meaning a semi-rural property that is just large enough to contain a house plus additional land which might support a few farm animals, or perhaps an orchard or small vineyard. Those who own such properties are often called lifestylers.

The word does appear on its own sometimes, to describe magazines, or particular kinds of shop, which are usually devoted to providing diversions with which the well-off can fill their time.

Q Lift

In the United States the term lift means shoes for short people or cosmetic surgery on the face. For New Zealanders, lift means a platform or compartment in a vertical shaft which carries goods or people. Americans stick to the more elaborate word, elevator.

Q Lippy

The Australian passion for abbreviation-plus-baby-talk has ensured that, across the Tasman, lipstick has become lippy. The term established itself in Australia about 1950.

Although New Zealanders understand the Australian use when they hear it, they tend towards the much older American use of the same word to mean boastful, arrogant, insolent and brash. This use has been fairly common in the United States since the mid-19th century. There is a subtle distinction between being insolent — lippy — and simply being too talkative. For the latter New Zealanders usually say mouthy.

Q Live

This term was used by television to indicate that something was actually happening at the moment that you saw it on-screen. Since this description was deemed to add value, the word's application has sneakily been widened to the stage where it is shamelessly used to describe anything seen anywhere, live or recorded. A New Zealand television series recorded on Fridays was regularly transmitted over 24 hours later and actually called 'Saturday Night Live'.

The opening ceremony of the 2000 Olympic Games was widely promoted in advance as live coverage, and commentators, promotions and advance print information reinforced the claim. New Zealanders discovered, however, that the transmission was *not* live, but videotaped and delayed. The ire of viewers grew to be great, not so much because the coverage was videotaped but because they'd been lied to and treated like idiots.

One partner of the word live has, thankfully, been abandoned: the slogan 'Recorded in front of a live audience' (to demonstrate that reactions and applause were not being fed off a taped track). The production moguls eventually realised that such a thing as a dead audience was most unlikely, and quietly removed the unnecessary adjective 'live' from the sentence.

Q Log of wood

A fanciful nickname since approximately 1930 for the inter-provincial rugby trophy, the Ranfurly Shield (which doesn't look anything like a log of wood, more like a shield!). The province winning the shield is known as the log-holder.

The Ranfurly Shield is named after Uchter Knox, who was officially Viscount Northland, Baron Wells of Dungannon and Earl of Ranfurly. He had a real silver-spoon background (Lord in Waiting to Queen Victoria) and was Governor of New Zealand from 1897 to 1904. Although he was known as a bossy governor who rapped ministers over the knuckles when he thought it necessary, the government admired him and the public held him in great affection.

As patron of the New Zealand Rugby Football Union, he presented the Ranfurly Shield in 1902, so to this day his title can cause wild emotions. (The trophy wouldn't have sounded quite as great had it been called the Uchter Knox Shield.)

Q Lolly

Obviously a shortened form of lollipop (which itself is derived from an ancient dialect word meaning tongue), the word lolly, sometimes spelt lollie, has been a widespread and preferred New Zealand term for almost any kind of confectionery since 1860. In general, its ancestor, lollipop, was used only for one specific form of sweetmeat: a toffee-like circle on a stick.

These and all other forms of lollies were bought out of a lolly jar at a lolly shop and put into a lolly bag. Occasionally, as a special treat, this could be accompanied by a bottle of lolly water (curiously, also known as soft drink, though its consistency is exactly the same as most other forms of drink!). Sometimes a slightly coarser alternative is used — chews. British people visiting New Zealand found the words lolly and chews mildly eccentric, since the common word in their homeland was simply sweets. Similarly, although the word candy is recognised in New

Zealand it is usually regarded as an American word.

(Beware, however, of toss your lollies: it means to vomit.)

Q Long drop

A design for a flush toilet was actually invented in 1775 but it was over 100 years before the facility became available for common usage. In the era before the device was available in New Zealand, and in districts where it still isn't available, two kinds of outdoor toilet developed.

One involved a seat fitted to a generous-sized metal can which was emptied at intervals, maybe even by the night-cart man who, during darkness, took away what was discreetly referred to as night soil.

The alternative was to dig a very, very deep hole, add a seat and erect a little building over it. Formally, this was known as a deep trench latrine or earth closet, but in popular parlance it was (and still is) called a long drop.

Q Loo

Its origin is unclear (perhaps the French *lieux d'aisance*, water closet), but in New Zealand loo joins the noble legion of word-substitutes for lavatory: restroom, bog, crapper, grot, dunny, head, shouse, WC, khasi, la-la, outhouse, long drop and, very rarely, the privy, the can or the john.

Q Lux

The electric suction sweeper was invented by J. Murray Spangler in Ohio, during the early 1900s. He didn't have much skill at marketing, and sought the advice of a nearby luggage maker called Hoover. Mr Hoover brought great success to the invention, so much so that many people thought he'd actually invented it himself. The electric suction sweeper gradually became known as a vacuum cleaner, and thousands were made with Mr Hoover's name on them. This gave rise to the terms 'hoovering' and 'the hoover', both of which can still be heard.

The Hoover brand did not seem to catch on in New Zealand as freely as the Electrolux, which became prominent. So, as well as people doing the vacuuming or the hoovering, the verb 'to lux' developed, and is still used in some districts at the beginning of the 21st century. The appliance itself, in those circumstances, is referred to as the lux.

Mad as a gumdigger's dog

During this country's early colonial days, kauri tree gum was an immensely important commodity. (Before the invention of plastics and vinyl, gum had many uses, one of which was as an ingredient of the floor covering called linoleum.)

'Gumdigger' features in several expressions that evolved in that era: gumdigger's soap (a certain kind of flower that lathered when scrunched up), gumdigger's spud (the edible bulb of a New Zealand orchid) and the ubiquitous gumdigger's dog. It is not possible to nail down exactly when or why the dogs came into disrepute, but it isn't difficult to picture living conditions among isolated groups of men camping on swampland for long periods of time. Neither the men nor their dogs would be examples of sleekness or elegance. Dogs are capable of fierce loyalty and ardent foraging, so a combination of all these factors is the probable origin of the three phrases that survive: skinny as a gumdigger's dog, useless as a gumdigger's dog and mad (meaning silly) as a gumdigger's dog.

 Maimai

This name for a little makeshift hut gives the impression of being a Maori word, but it isn't. Australian scholars trace it to the Nyungar language of Aboriginals in Western Australia. Peter Carey's novel *True History of the Kelly Gang* has the notorious Ned Kelly using the word (spelled miamia) in approximately 1870 to describe a shelter 'such as the blackfellows build'.

Versions of the word have occurred in New Zealand since the 1860s when Europeans observed the Maori custom of building

shelters from sticks covered with hastily woven raupo and fern —
though it was the Europeans using the Australian word, not the
Maori (who may have preferred their own word, whare).

After the discovery of gold in New Zealand, when prospectors
were reluctant to leave a riverside, they quickly learnt the craft of
building a maimai for themselves, and during the First World
War New Zealand troops used the word at Gallipoli. Since the
1930s, passionate duck-shooters, too, have built maimais near
water, partly for shelter and partly for concealment.

The Mainland

This is a common term for the South Island of New Zealand.
Since it is the biggest of the islands that form New Zealand,
theoretically it is the main island and all the others are subsidiary.
In early colonial times New Zealand's South Island was certainly
a busy mainspring of prosperity (though not politics — New
Zealand's four successive capitals have always been in the north),
so it is possible that the term Mainland was 'understood' for
decades before going into popular parlance.

The term was certainly known to Field Marshal Lord
Montgomery who, when touring New Zealand after the Second
World War, made a memorable speech at King Edward Barracks
in Christchurch, during which his reference to the South Island
as the Mainland was greeted with enthusiastic applause. A legend
has grown that this occasion, in 1947, was the first public utterance
of the term.

Subsequently, Canterbury-born Sir Sidney Holland used the
term frequently during his time as Prime Minister (1949–1957).
By 1960 the term Mainland was recognisable to most New
Zealanders as meaning the South Island, though sometimes, when
said, it was accompanied by a slightly wry expression.

Mall

Groups of shops all in a row, facing another group of shops all in a row, with a no-vehicle walking area in between, have been around for a very long time, called arcades. (London has its Burlington Arcade, and there are several smaller but similar examples in the New Zealand cities.) But in the 1950s shopping centres began to be built in a cluster shape with generous parking space, and eventually a very old word was called back into use to describe them.

The word mall is derived from the Italian phrase *palla a maglio*, which is the name of an old mallet-and-ball game. When the game, and its name, reached England it was anglicised to become pall mall.

The game began to fade from popularity, but left two legacies in English: the phrase pell-mell, meaning fast and vigorous (like the game), and the names of places where it used to be played — Pall Mall and the street called The Mall. In the absence of the noisy game, London's Mall became a rather elegant street, and the word mall developed the connotation of green grass and pleasant walking.

In 1967 the word mall was used to refer to a shopping centre in the United States and now it is common everywhere.

New Zealanders decline to observe its transition through England when pronouncing the word. In London, if you ask directions to 'Pawl Mawl' you'll be met with a blank stare. Pall Mall rhymes with gal and that's that. In New Zealand it is universally pronounced to rhyme with brawl.

Malvina

In New Zealand the name is firmly associated with one national living treasure, opera singer Dame Malvina Major. Attractive though the name is, it doesn't crop up very often — the composer of 'Morningtown Ride' has it, the Falklands Islands prefer it and a secretary in Washington was also once called Malvina. It was she who played a small role in New Zealand's musical destiny.

Dame Malvina tells that, before she was born, her father one night read out an item from the newspaper regarding Eleanor Roosevelt. His wife took less notice of the news than of a brief mention of Mrs Roosevelt's secretary in Washington, who was called Malvina. 'Nice name,' thought Mrs Major and tucked the name aside for when her baby was born.

As Dame Malvina Major's fame grew, she experienced an amusing incident concerning her name. Inspired by her singing, a company in Australia suggested to her that the musical sound of Malvina would be a delightful name for a new range of wine they were marketing. As is usual, the word was put through language checks to ensure its marketability worldwide. The answer didn't make one jot of difference to Malvina Major's singing career, but it did mean that no vineyard crop was named after her — unfortunately, in all Spanish-speaking countries, *mal vina* could easily be interpreted as bad wine.

 Mana

As with many Maori words, no single English word equates exactly with the term mana. The closest designation would be prestige, with a strong inclusion of dignity, and very often power and influence as well.

The quality of mana may be possessed by an individual person or by a group (as in an aristocratic family or an assembly of high-ranking government officials). It is not actually bestowed but accumulates subtly over time. The presence of mana in a person or a position is often visibly demonstrated — for instance by their physical placing in events of ordered ritual. Thus, although the prestige and rank of a person of mana are clearly recognised by all observers, it is not usually self-claimed or self-acknowledged.

Maori

Maori are the indigenous Polynesian people of New Zealand. There is some doubt as to what the word originally meant, scholars pointing to 'normal people' as the most probable since, having lived centuries in comparative isolation, most Maori were unaware of other races or of any need to have a word specifically to describe themselves. Maori somehow escaped the epithet of either Aboriginals or Indians, both terms used elsewhere. Visitors having trouble aligning the look of the word to its correct pronunciation could be discreetly advised to think 'mowrie'.

 Maori bread

Usually made with fermented potato-yeast, Maori bread is one of the most delicious taste treats imaginable. It is known by various names, especially rewena, and it must be eaten very fresh.

Q **Maori strum**

This distinctive style of playing guitar accompaniments seems to belong only to Maori musicians. The strum consists of two hits on each beat (one up, one down) with a slight bounce. The two hits are separated 'as if they were a triplet with a hole in the middle' (according to eminent guitarist Martin Winch) and 'with beat 2 and beat 4 being accented and short'.

Any New Zealander can recognise the result, which is a slightly syncopated rhythm. Music star Neil Finn describes the sound as 'ah ching ker chik'. (Repeat that phrase over several times and you'll get the general idea.)

In addition to the shape of that characteristic strum, the harmonies utilised also frequently have a Maori sound, based on a liking for chords with an open 6th in them, either in addition to, or in preference to, the traditional triad, which would include a 5th but not a 6th.

Maori time

Most New Zealanders recognise that Maori perceive the passage of time in a way that doesn't always mesh with the European concept. Mentioning such a matter can be attacked as politically incorrect so it may be wise to explain the concept by using only the words of the late Professor Ernest Beaglehole, anthropologist and philosopher, written in 1948 before political correctness was invented:

'The modern Maori adapts himself to two concepts of time. One is the Pakeha concept: time is something solid, fixed and definite, to which other activities must be geared. You adapt to Pakeha time when you want to catch a bus badly enough, go to the pictures, or knock off work at the end of the day.

'Maori time, on the other hand, is a plastic medium that flows around and adapts itself to the activities of the day. The Maori time for anything is when you are ready to do it. A Pakeha hostess may become worried if her guests do not arrive on time. Not so the Maori hostess. Food will be ready to eat whenever anyone is ready to eat it.

'It is not that the Maori does not have clocks about the house with which to order his life. Most houses have a clock, generally accurate enough for buses and pictures, as long as you remember that the clock is probably "so much" fast or slow.

'Pakeha time is a sort of necessary nuisance, to which you adapt, to be able to do other desirable things.'

Q Marae

To a casual observer a marae is merely a piece of land with an open central area surrounded by several buildings, one of which is likely to be a wharenui or meeting house, with a peaked roof and dramatic carvings. The word marae strictly refers only to the open piece of land in front of the wharenui, though modern general usage tends to describe the whole complex of buildings and land (slightly incorrectly) as a marae.

A marae is used for meetings and social occasions such as parties and weddings, but its significance is far greater. Although it does not always show constant ritual, the marae fulfils a particular purpose in Maori tradition: it is a centre of tribal (family) life, and its ceremonial aspects can be invoked when the occasion warrants — a formal welcome to people from another district (so their feet have a place on strange ground), a tangi or funeral, or a vigorous formally structured meeting where, by long-standing custom, the truth must be told and honest opinion must be expressed.

In European terms a marae sits somewhere between a parliament, a church and a village green, seamlessly manifesting elements of all three at different times.

Q Marching girls

It's moderately difficult to believe that New Zealand invented marching girls but it seems to be true. They were first noticed in 1901, when assembled to perform for a royal visit. In those days the activity was called girls' drill. Within 20 years the activity had become organised as a sport and grew even more prolific during the Depression years. Marching did not require many resources, expensive equipment or huge areas of land, and it provided congenial activity, exercise and competition and (in its time) won respectful attention. In smart but glamorous uniforms the girls marched expertly through complex, accurate and entertaining patterns. The sport flourished.

The first competitions were held in 1933 and the New Zealand Marching and Recreation Association was formed in 1945 to set codes of rules and costume.

There were critics — some commentators said the uniformed and briskly marching girls were merely playing soldiers — but in 1952 the Blair Athol team from New Zealand gave performances in England and Scotland and amazed everyone with their 'femininity'. There were over 350 teams of marching girls by 1980 and television featured nationwide coverage of the national final competitions.

Soon after that, the concept and the enthusiastic participation both cooled. A more eclectic era offered other forms of leisure and the peak number of marching girl participants in New Zealand (over 6000) dwindled. The form survives, now somewhat influenced by American drum majorettes and reverting to the name of 100 years earlier: marching girls are now called drill teams.

 ## Margarine

A silent revolution took place in New Zealand during the 1970s, when margarine crept onto supermarket shelves and became as easily available as butter. Margarine was first developed in France, and was patented in the United States in 1873. To the health conscious, one of its major attractions is that it can be made entirely from plant oils (though not always: in Europe, whale oil has frequently been used). The word margarine comes from the Greek word *margaron*, meaning pearl, which real margarine resembles before being dyed yellow to look like butter.

The name Margaret has the same origin — a pearl among women.

 ## Marrow

Though it can mean the fatty tissue filling the cavities in the middle of bones, in New Zealand the word marrow also means a long substantial vegetable, usually green with light orange spots or stripes. Elsewhere it is known as squash.

 ## Mate

Visitors to New Zealand and Australia are sometimes faintly puzzled at hearing mate said in an unfamiliar context. In formal and clinical terms 'to mate' generally means that you intend to produce children — it is the common term for animals who have maternity in view and a mate is a permanent partner usually of the opposite sex.

In New Zealand this is not necessarily so. Although the formal meaning still applies to animals and birds, the more frequent use of the word applies to a habitual companion or close friend —the person who could be known elsewhere as a buddy, a chum or a pal. And while sex doesn't come into it, the mates being referred to are generally both male. Discount prices on money transactions between friends or family are referred to as mates' rates.

'Mate!' said in isolation can indicate strong endorsement and approval. But, said another way, the word can convey an ironic contradiction to any sense of friendship: 'The door's locked and you're not coming in, mate.'

All these uses are originally British and not new. In 1861 Charles Dickens conveyed all the connotations in the line: 'This what you're lying on, mate, is Tom Tiddler's ground.'

 ## Meat safe

The word is seldom heard in post-refrigeration years but in former times every kitchen revolved around it and some isolated bush huts still use it. A meat safe was a box-like cupboard (either mounted separately outside, or actually built into the house design) in the coolest situation, with one side or one wall panel fitted with fine wire netting to allow air in but keep flies out. The netting was sometimes fitted with wooden angle-slatting to prevent sunlight getting in.

Meat and other perishable comestibles were kept in this, the coolest situation that could be found for them. Flies were the big danger — even one inadvertently shut inside would render the entire contents of the safe unhygienic. A folklore custom supposedly solved that: allow a spider to live inside the safe and it would keep the food safe!

Q Messages

'Doing the messages' is New Zealand shorthand for quick, necessary shopping, buying the household's daily needs. It often strikes visitors as a quaint turn of phrase although, to New Zealand ears, doing the errands or the marketing sounds equally quaint.

Q Metal

Although metal obviously means chemical elements that are usually solid, or alloys of these, the word also has a subsidiary meaning: naturally occurring rocks and stones which, when crushed and broken, form the surface of unsealed country roads. Hence they can be referred to as metal roads.

This use of the word puzzles visitors to New Zealand, who find the term metal road confusing. A Britisher in rural New Zealand once remarked that she had reached a particular destination by travelling on an unmade road. Her host, slightly offended, pointed out with slight firmness that the road *was* made. It just didn't have a sealed surface — it was a metal road.

Q Metathesis

An Auckland woman, describing an illness, said her neighbour had 'gone bald because of *appalachia*'. Although this is actually a malapropism (she meant alopecia), it is also an example of metathesis: the formal term for transposing two parts of a word. This is particularly common in New Zealand where, for some unknown reason, the beginning and ends of words remain stable, but the sounds or syllables in the middle are often inverted.

For instance, the word ask comes from an ancient English word *ascian*, so the 's' has come before the 'c' for several hundred years. But many New Zealanders challenge the tradition, relentlessly turning the word back-to-front and pronouncing it as *aks*.

So also a dais is often called a *dias*, a secretary becomes a *secertary*, an asterisk is pronounced as *asteriks*, relevant hides behind *revelant* and integral behind *intregal*. Anemones transmute into *anenomes*, anonymous frequently adds a further disguise by being *anomynous*, and mother-of-pearl iridescence turns into *irisidence*.

New Zealand's historical association with colonisation sometimes comes out as *conolisation*, the district of Hanmer becomes *Hamner* (though curiously, Sumner never becomes *Sunmer*), child prodigies often become *pogidies* and there is great consciousness about being *nucular*-free rather than nuclear-free. A politician is heard on radio saying that he has been *unindated* with letters (though presumably he was inundated).

It happens with Maori words too: Manurewa sometimes comes out as *Manuwera*, Waiwera can be mangled into *Wairewa* and Moutoa Gardens is consistently reversed into *Motua* Gardens.

There was a field day for metathesis towards the end of the year 2000, when millennium often became *minnellium* and pedants felt particularly *vunlerable*. Sorry, vulnerable.

Milk bottle

A milk bottle made of glass has almost become a historic artifact of New Zealand social history. The traditional milk carrier called a billy (a cylinder-shaped container, usually of white enamel, with a wire handle, sometimes lidded, sometimes not) was gradually replaced by glass bottles, which held sway — at least in city areas — for many decades. Milk in bottles was customarily bought at the corner dairy or the empty bottles were left at the front gate overnight, with money inside them, and during the night a milkman took the bottles and the money and left new glass bottles filled with milk.

New Zealanders who went to school between 1937 and 1967 were accustomed to a free half-pint of milk a day, given to every school child — in a glass bottle. From 1940 to 1945 that was joined by a free apple for every pupil.

But starting in 1987 milk became available in cardboard containers and the use of those became widespread. Later containers of thin plastic arrived. (These are sometimes still called milk bottles although they are deliberately shaped like flagons.) In the northern parts of the country, by the 1990s, most young people had never heard the term 'milk bottle' and milkmen had become as rare as gas lamplighters.

 Moa

Correctly known as *Dinornithiformes*, moa were large flightless birds of ancient ancestry, in existence 15 million years ago and probably earlier. They occurred through all the main parts of New Zealand, grazing on grasses, leaves and fruit.

Early human inhabitants of New Zealand hunted the birds for food, used their bones for implements and their eggshells for water bottles (their eggs were up to 25 centimetres long). Over an estimated 500 years, the moa population was culled to near-invisibility. In early colonial times, the moa held a fanciful place as a national emblem and nearly supplanted the kiwi. The kiwi won, possibly because its fading away was arrested and its existence encouraged. Live kiwi can still be seen. Nobody has seen a living moa since about 1500.

 Moko

Although moko in Maori means tattoo, it also means lizard and it is not difficult to see the connection when you examine the usual style of Maori tattooing.

Maori facial and body tattooing followed, and still follows, strictly observed rituals and designs. A line of ancestry, a rank by blood, family and legendary connections — all can be portrayed within the intricate designs. And, if questioned, anyone bearing the lines of a particular family or status had better be able to prove their justifiable right to do so. Maori moko patterns come very close to the European concept of copyright.

Money for jam

This expression is affiliated to 'money for old rope', which was a simple statement of truth: sailing-ship crews collected tattered bits of rope while at sea, then sold them on shore for caulking or plugging gaps. Collecting the rope required no effort so the profit was easy. Money for jam developed from this, for no clear reason, but equally meaning that profit could be made with little effort. For no clear reason either, New Zealanders stuck to the jam version, which is not widely heard elsewhere.

Morepork

The morepork, whose proper name is *Ninox novaeseelandiae*, is a small, brown, native owl. There is some difference of opinion as to what sound the bird makes. When Maori hear it, they hear ruru. Australians, hearing a similar bird, are convinced it is saying boo book. Early European settlers to New Zealand begged to differ: to their ears the bird was, enigmatically, calling morepork. They were calling it by that name even before the Treaty of Waitangi was signed in 1840.

Moreporks are not often seen, but their sound is not unknown to suburban dwellers. The birds are quite confident and will move into city parks or large garden trees. They eat insects and little meaty things like mice and lizards, or even small birds — but not, as far as anyone knows, pork.

Mother of all . . .

New Zealand became accustomed to the phrase in 1991, but it had been around for several hundred years before that. The concept appears to date back to the Muslim leader Mohammed, who was known as the father of all believers, his wife Ayesha being the mother of all believers, and thus an almost equally significant and important figure.

Various versions of this same concept have been in the English language for years: they appear to have started out as 'the mother and father of . . .' and then narrowed down to just mother. During the 19th century the phrase 'Mother of All Parliaments' arose to refer to the nation of Britain as a whole, not just to its parliament.

During the 1991 Gulf War, Saddam Hussein used the expression 'mother of all' in its original Muslim sense to describe, with some potency, the Iraqi force with which he would destroy invaders.

In the same year New Zealand Finance Minister Ruth Richardson used the expression to describe the National government's forthcoming budget. Her phrasing made such a media impact that the phrase 'mother of all' has remained in common use, indicating something powerfully big and more important than usual.

Muck around

This expression has its origin in an Old Norse word for dung, but the expression 'mucking around' has little to connect it with that. It is derived from the British term 'mucking about', meaning to be involved in useless activity (or rather, non-activity).

New Zealanders prefer the slight variation 'mucking around', where the term is used in two contexts: doing nothing in particular in a leisurely sense, or occupying time but not achieving anything where something should be achieved. This latter can be double-edged — if you're waiting while nothing happens because the person or organisation you want to speak to is inefficient and causing *you* to waste time, you are mucking around, because *they* are mucking around.

Mudguards

The curved metal shape that sits over and slightly away from car wheels, to prevent water and mud from being splashed upwards as the vehicle travels along, are sometimes called wings in other places.

Q Muttonbird

The term muttonbird is applied to the young of various seabirds, but mainly the sooty shearwater and the grey-faced petrel. The flesh, when cooking, has a mutton-like smell. The first known mention in English was in 1823 when a writer described a Maori chief's trip to Stewart Island to stock up for the winter on muttonbirds (a term that Maori themselves couldn't possibly have used at the time, since sheep were unknown to them). Muttonbirds has remained the English-given name ever since.

The birds were (and still are) cooked in their own fat, which was sufficient to preserve them as well, for trading to other parts of the country. Always considered as a delicacy, the muttonbirds became a special treat for the 28th Maori Battalion during the Second World War, when their womenfolk back home packed large quantities and sent them to soldiers in North Africa. The traitor broadcaster Lord Haw-Haw heard about this and, anxious to undermine Allied morale, announced on the radio that the New Zealand troops were so short of food that they were eating salted seagulls. The Maori soldiers, thoroughly enjoying their much-travelled treat, roared with laughter, of course.

(The birds also turned up somewhat unexpectedly as the name of a New Zealand music group, The Muttonbirds, whose popularity began in 1991.)

Q Nappy

This is an abbreviation for napkin, but not the kind used at elegant dinner parties. Unlike the United States, where babies are kept clean by being folded into diapers (derived from a mediaeval Greek word meaning pure white — a word use of touching faith in this particular case), New Zealand has stuck with napkin to name the same accessory, and typically abbreviated it to nappy or nap.

Apart from normal development (such as the modern disposable nappies), at least one other extension has occurred. In 1972 visiting British writer Austin Mitchell reported that suburbs containing many young households with babies were jokingly referred to by their inhabitants as Nappy Valley.

Q National Anthem

In 1840 New Zealand's national anthem was established as 'God Save the Queen' and will remain so as long as the nation is a kingdom. It must be played if the sovereign or a representative thereof is physically present.

But New Zealand has two national anthems. Thomas Bracken, an Irishman living in Dunedin, wrote the words of 'God Defend New Zealand', which was published as a poem in 1876. An enthusiastic nationalist, Bracken set up a competition to find a tune for his words, the winner being John Joseph Woods of Lawrence. The resulting song became very popular and although Bracken boldly printed it with the words 'National Anthem' on the cover, it really wasn't. Nevertheless, people throughout the country sang the song and by 1878 Sir George Grey was suggesting that a Maori version be organised. This is heard more in the 21st century than it was in the 19th or 20th.

By 1940 the song had become unavoidable and the government bought the copyright and established 'God Defend' as a national song. (A national anthem can only be sanctioned by the sovereign.)

Growing pressure caused high-level discussions within Parliament and consultation with the sovereign who, in 1977, agreed to the establishing of 'God Defend New Zealand' as the second national anthem, which can be used on national occasions when the sovereign is not present. Paradoxically, as soon as the anthem became official, it began to wane in popularity. Complaints about its Victorian idealism and heavy-footed tune wore down the 100 years of enthusiasm that caused its elevated status. Cries to get rid of the song began to be heard.

Nobody is sure what the phrase, 'Guard Pacific's triple star', refers to: New Zealand's original three provinces, the three main islands, a misprint . . . ? Nobody knows.

GOD DEFEND NEW ZEALAND

God of nations, at Thy feet
In the bonds of love we meet
Hear our voices we entreat,
God defend our free land.
Guard Pacific's triple star
From the shafts of strife and war
Make our praises heard afar,
God defend New Zealand.

Men of every creed and race
Gather here before Thy face
Asking Thee to bless this place,
God defend our free land.
From dissension, envy, hate
And corruption guard our state
Make our country good and great,
God defend New Zealand.

147

Peace, not war shall be our boast
But, should foes assail our coast
Make us then a mighty host,
God defend our free land.
Lord of battles in Thy might
Put our enemies to flight
Let our cause be just and right
God defend New Zealand.

Let our love for Thee increase
May Thy blessings never cease
Give us plenty, give us peace
God defend our free land.
From dishonour and from shame
Guard our country's spotless name
Crown her with immortal fame,
God defend New Zealand.

May our mountains ever be
Freedom's ramparts on the sea
Make us faithful unto Thee,
God defend our free land.
Guide her in the nations' van
Preaching love and truth to man
Working out Thy glorious plan
God defend New Zealand.

E Ihoa Atua
O nga iwi matou ra
Ata whakarongo na,
Me aroha noa
Kia hua ko te pai
Kia tau to atawhai,
Manaakitia mai
Aotearoa.

Q Next

The word's exact meaning is immediately adjacent, but within the broadcasting industry of New Zealand, a different meaning has developed: next means after the commercials.

Q Nibbles

For New Zealanders, nibbles are small food items on trays or in bowls offered at a social function where no actual meal is being served. Except in formal situations (or on restaurant menus), New Zealanders tend to bypass the words used by other cultures (antipasto, canapés, crudités, hors d'oeuvres) in favour of nibbles or sometimes finger food, meaning that a knife and fork (and often a plate) are not required.

Q Niggly

To be niggly is to be impatient, critical, short-tempered, fractious, fussy. The New Zealand fondness for abbreviation could suggest that niggly is a shortened form of niggardly, but this is not the case: the two words are different in both origin and meaning, though both were originally Scandinavian. Niggardly, which indicates miserliness about money or being grudging with activity or generosity, comes from the Swedish word *nygg*, indicating stinginess. Niggly is derived from a Norwegian word, *nigla*.

Q No-hoper

Fairly self-explanatory, the term has been shared between New Zealand and Australia since the 1940s, and means a person who is ineffectual, incompetent and for whom (in a rather exaggerated sense) there is no hope.

149

Q No kidding?

Although kid means a young goat, and has done for several hundred years, the related term kidding, meaning joking and teasing, arose early in the 19th century. It arose, so scholars believe, as an imitative term, because of young goats' tendency to frisk about while maintaining an impertinent look on their faces.

Hence by 1811, particularly in the United States, kidding was bantering deception, and the phrase 'Are you kidding me?' meant 'Are you telling the strict truth?'

By 1873 this had shortened to 'No kid?', meaning the same thing, but curiously it was a middle-length version that caught on in New Zealand. The remark 'no kidding' is usually a question ('Are you telling the truth?') but on some occasions can be used as a statement ('I'm telling the truth').

Q 'Now is the Hour'

'Now is the Hour' is promoted as being a proud native of New Zealand, although the tune is from Australia. It was composed in Sydney by the musician A.B. Saunders (who used the pen name Clement Scott) and was published in 1913 as a piano solo called 'Swiss Cradle Song'. At that time the tune was in gentle 4/4 with no words.

When it drifted across the Tasman, Maori musicians changed it to waltz time and several versions of Maori words were fitted to it. Part-Maori musician Maewa Kaihau tidied up the Maori words in time for the 1920 visit by the Prince of Wales, to whom the song was sung. By 1929 it had an English translation, and the name 'Now is the Hour'.

In 1936 American preacher J. Edwin Orr, touring New Zealand, heard the song and wrote it out on a scrap of paper. He wrote Christian words for it, and 'Now is the Hour' became widely published and circulated in the United States as 'Search Me, O God'.

'Now is the Hour' received its greatest boost internationally when British mega-star Gracie Fields visited New Zealand in 1945 and learnt the song. Gracie knew a good song when she heard it, and once she got back to England, she arranged to record 'Now is the Hour' in 1947. It became a huge hit, both in Britain and the United States. A chartered aircraft was required to carry 5 tons of the record across the Atlantic to the States and the ship *Queen Mary* followed with a further 10 tons.

After Gracie Fields' version, the song was recommended to Bing Crosby, whose version went onto the American hit parades early in 1948 and became a million seller. Some years later, Frank Sinatra recorded an album called 'Great Songs from Great Britain' which, by some research error, included 'Now is the Hour'.

In 1999 Dame Kiri Te Kanawa set the matter straight by recording the song, only in the Maori language, to make it clear to the rest of the world where the song's main significance rested.

No worries

Essentially an expression that arose in Australia, it has become popular and widely used on both sides of the Tasman. Although no worries means exactly what it says, it demonstrates grammatical ellipsis or shorthand: the speaker is indicating confidence and competence that he or she can accomplish a task with ease.

Nugget

Actually meaning a small lump of something in its natural state (e.g. gold, coal, gum), the word is frequently used as an adjective — nuggety — to describe a person or animal who is stocky of build and not tall.

In 1903 the London-based Nugget Polish Company filed a patent to sell their leather preservative in New Zealand. There is no formal explanation for the name — the reason was probably because it was originally black and sold in lumps. When it was tinned, the lid showed a picture of a glittering black nugget.

Within a decade nugget had become a normal term in New Zealand for shoe polish, joining the list of trade names that moved into common language, and the verb 'to nugget' was coined, meaning to polish one's shoes, even when using another brand. Brown polish was later added to the original black, giving rise to the informal descriptions nugget brown and nugget black, even of commodities that had nothing to do with shoe polish.

Number eight (No. 8) wire

Wire comes in different thicknesses, differentiated by a gauge and a number. As the number goes higher, the wire gets thicker and stronger. For many years in New Zealand, a straight piece of No. 12 wire, thick and strong, could be sharpened into a good fishing spear. But the favoured wire for New Zealand fencing was No. 8. Because of its predominance for this work, the wire was very commonly available and had a good reputation for strength. Hence, it became useful for temporarily fixing other things, particularly mechanical, or for holding something together firmly. In time the phrase 'No. 8 fencing wire' became a byword for making an ingenious repair with materials close to hand.

In the 21st century, fencing wire has become high-tech and high-tensile and the classic No. 8 is seen much less frequently in an emergency than plastic twine. But the phrase, No. 8 wire, remains as a symbolic equivalent of the more modern DIY.

O

 Oceania

New Zealanders customarily refer to the geographic area around them as the Pacific or, at a pinch, the South Pacific. There was a move in the 1960s to have New Zealanders refer to themselves as part of South-East Asia, but it never really took off. A large portion of the rest of the world calmly refers to this geographic area as Oceania, a term many New Zealanders have never heard, let alone used.

By (fairly loose) definition, Oceania means the islands of the central and South Pacific, including Melanesia, Polynesia and Micronesia, sometimes also including Australia and the Malay Archipelago.

The term is commonly used throughout Europe in somewhat unexpected situations — when posting a parcel to New Zealand, for instance, the price of postage will be listed under the area Oceania rather than South Pacific. Americans, often fairly vague about geography, have only a woolly idea of where anywhere in the Pacific is and tend to think South Pacific means Hawaii (it's not, Hawaii is in the *North* Pacific) and in general are unfamiliar with the word Oceania.

The term crops up in the collective name for a sporting event (Oceania Games) but is seldom seen elsewhere on its home territory. Anyone saying to a New Zealander, 'Oh, you're from Oceania,' is likely to receive a blank look in return.

Q Odd

Besides meaning not divisible by two, odd has other applications:

(1) unusual, peculiar as in 'He was an *odd* person, who behaved a little bit strangely'.

(2) random, occasional, as in 'After the knitting was finished, some odd bits of wool were left over'.

It is this latter meaning that is embraced in New Zealand. Weather reports predict that there will be odd showers, which doesn't mean peculiar showers, but unpredictable and occasional rain. A person who experiences the odd spot of bother lands into trouble from time to time.

Q OE

Living in a geographically isolated country, New Zealanders have long nurtured two conflicting urges — first, that the country and its inhabitants are self-sufficient, unheeding of and unwilling to adopt the practices and rhythms of other cultures and, second, a curiosity and reluctant attraction towards what happens and is admired overseas.

Since the mid-19th century, many New Zealanders have sought to travel beyond the Pacific to witness first-hand how the other portion of the world lives. Some yearn to do so and never come back (witness Katherine Mansfield). Some come back gratefully, rejoicing in space, clean air and lack of oppressive pressure. They have had their OE: overseas experience. If the overseas experience extends to a year or more, it is frequently called the big OE.

The phenomenon is not at all new, nor is it confined to New Zealanders. During past centuries, Britishers who could afford to, customarily went on what was called a Grand Tour, visiting the art galleries and the social whirl of nations on the Continent (which to a New Zealander seem curiously nearby to Britain, rather than distant). But their travel did not involve backpacking, hitchhiking, Youth Hostels and crossing India in clapped-out motor vehicles, which New Zealanders' OE often does.

Offshore

In the past, the principal meaning of offshore was somewhere out in the water, maybe not too far from the beach. Fishing lines and oil rigs were offshore. This meaning still applies, but the word has also evolved an extra use.

For some reason, New Zealanders developed a reluctance to say the word 'foreign' and the much-used 'overseas' began to sound naive. So offshore had its meaning extended and slowly became another way of saying on land (but in another country).

Thus, items being manufactured offshore, or business funds being invested offshore, could mean just out in the harbour — or in Taiwan or Russia.

 Old boy

Men, who in their youth all went to the same school, call themselves old boys of that institution. Americans would call them male alumni. Sometimes, as a gesture towards age-sensitivity, the terms ex-student or ex-pupil are used to replace old boy andold girl.

The old boy network refers to a system by which information or advantageous business insights are exchanged among those who share bonds of loyalty from school or university days. This approach replaces more usual formal channels.

Ombudsman

In 1962 the New Zealand government introduced the office of Ombudsman into the country's social structure. The word is Swedish and translates as agent or commissioner, which doesn't explain much.

The Ombudsman is an officer of Parliament who investigates complaints by individuals against government agencies such as ministries and departments (which does not include the legal decisions of courts). If the Ombudsman decides that some unfairness or inefficiency has occurred, he or she delivers a decision to that effect. There is no power to order government officials to do anything, only to offer recommendations. But, 99 per cent of the time, the advice is acted upon.

Other organisations such as banking and insurance have set up similar structures, but the Chief Ombudsman is the main source of hope for unrest about the action of a government department.

Q On the knocker

Meaning punctual, prompt, accurate, like a hinged brass ornament firmly rat-tat-tatting on a door, the expression is believed to originate in New Zealand and Australia. But a little caution is needed: on the knocker (singular) is fine, but should the knocker become plural — knockers — you're speaking of a womanly bosom, and rather offensively.

Q Operation

This medical process, by which any part of the body is manipulated or accessed to repair damage, halt disease or alter in some way, is often called surgery elsewhere, but New Zealanders will generally say they are entering hospital for an operation rather than for surgery.

Q Opo

For a short space of time in the summer of 1955–1956, Opo became New Zealand's favourite word. It was the name given to a bottle-nosed dolphin living near Opononi in Northland. Holidaymakers at the seaside resort that summer were astonished at Opo's friendly nature and accessibility. She frolicked and leapt and played with swimming children and very quickly became so famous that journalists compared her to an ancient Roman dolphin called Hippo, who had similarly played with swimming children in the year AD 100. Opo was protected by a New Zealand Government Order-in-Council taking effect at midnight on 8 March 1956. Sadly, she was found dead only a few hours later, on 9 March. Crombie Murdoch's song 'Opo the Crazy Dolphin', recorded by Pat McMinn, cemented the creature into Kiwi folklore and in Opononi a charming Russell Clark sculpture commemorates the dolphin herself.

 ## Orange roughy

This curious name belongs to a once popular eating fish, correctly called *Hoplostethus atlanticus*. The term sprang into prominence when a russet-haired female MP suddenly sported a new shaggy hairstyle, and the prime minister of the time, asked what he thought of it, said simply, 'Orange roughy'.

 ## Oz

The word first appeared in print in 1900. American author L. Frank Baum created a fantasy tale about a girl called Dorothy and her friends the Tin Man, the Cowardly Lion and the Scarecrow. They were heading for a magical mystical place, reached by travelling down a yellow brick road. Legend has it that Baum, seeking a name for their destination, noticed that two huge encyclopaedias on his study shelf were marked, on the spines, A–N and O–Z. Bingo: he had found a short, sharp, exotic name. His book was published as *The Wonderful Wizard of Oz*.

For many decades, when referring to Australia, New Zealanders used the abbreviated term Aussie, which meant either the country itself, or the people who lived there. Over time, Baum's shorter word came into favour, and Aussie became abbreviated again, to Oz. This usually refers to the country; the inhabitants are still called Aussies or, fairly rarely, an Oz.

(An Australian is also occasionally described as an Ocker, a nonsense word derived from a character's name in an Australian comedy TV series.)

P

 Pack a sad

Although pack has its usual meanings associated with loading things into a definite existing space, it also surfaces in New Zealand when associated with a state of depression.

The expression 'pack a sad' came into currency about 1980 and was initially applied to anyone who was upset, seeking help and sympathy, or remaining silent in the face of depressing news.

Gradually, by extension, the term came to be applied to non-human situations where something incapable of actually feeling sadness (the weather, a car, a domestic appliance) went into a state of malfunction or a condition causing displeasure and was also said to pack a sad.

 Paddock

Paddock is derived from the English dialect word *parroc*, meaning an area of open land which is fenced (it also survives in park). In Britain, the word is usually associated with horse-racing activity rather than farming. In Australia and New Zealand, although paddock is also used for horse activities, it features far more frequently in farm contexts, since New Zealanders tend to resist saying meadow or field.

Pakaru

The Maori word pakaru, meaning broken, ruined, not able to function, was very quickly taken up by Europeans who heard it.

Pakaru first appeared in 1820 in an English-language report from New Zealand. Because some spoken-Maori consonants do not match exactly with the English alphabet, there was some variance in how the English heard Maori people saying the word, so in the 19th century it was spelt in different ways: pakadu, pukeru, buckeroo and, most commonly, puckaroo.

The creeping in of what some Europeans thought was a b sound (see buckaroo, above) also led to a theory that pakaru was not a Maori word at all, but a Maori version of a word they'd heard the Europeans say — bugger. But there is no evidence to support this.

In contemporary times the word has settled down and is used in both languages, English and Maori, and has even become (in English) a verb — to be pakaru'd.

Maori people spell and pronounce pakaru in the Maori manner, with a pronunciation emphasis on the first syllable. Europeans tend to speak it as if it were spelt puckaroo.

 Pakeha

New Zealand residents or visitors who are not Polynesian are referred to as Pakeha. Initially used by Maori people identifying any pale-coloured stranger who was not one of themselves, the exact origin and meaning of the Maori word has been widely disputed and never satisfactorily clarified. Because some of the conjectured original meanings are in doubtful taste, use of the word — though relatively common — can be regarded as contentious, even offensive.

 Panel beater

Visitors from the United States have been known to take photographs of signs in New Zealand advertising a panel beater because, to them, it is such a funny word. By the same token, New Zealanders are amused at the American equivalent — body shop.

The reasoning behind both uses is equally valid. A car has a body that is made up of many joined panels. When one or other of the panels is damaged, you take it to an expert who, you hope, can recreate its original shape. Said expert probably operates out of a workshop, shortened to shop.

In New Zealand the term panel beater remains the accepted norm. Should a visitor ask directions to a body shop he might be sent, with a sideways look, to a murky part of town.

Parameter

The correct meaning of parameter is an arbitrary constant that determines the specific form of a mathematical expression. Very few people understand this, and the fact that the word sounds rather like perimeter could be the reason why many people use one when they mean the other.

Perimeter means the outside boundary, so to work within the perimeter of something makes sense. But parameter somehow sounds more learned, even if it's wrongly used. Common New Zealand usage places parameter as a substitute for many other words and phrases: boundaries, principles, guidelines, rules, range, limitations, policy, factors that can be changed, factors that can't be changed, assumptions, intentions, strengths and weaknesses, ideas, scope. It can even be stretched to mean vital organs — as once used in a news statement about Mother Teresa that mentioned 'her heart and other parameters'.

Passionfruit

The fruit's name has nothing to do with aphrodisiacs, but more with the structure of the spectacular flowers.

There are dozens of different kinds of passionfruit native to Brazil. Early Spanish Jesuit missionaries used the flowers of the vine to teach about the passion of Jesus. The corona represents the crown of thorns, the styles represent the nails used in the crucifixion, the stamens represent five wounds, and the five sepals and five petals represent 10 of the apostles — excluding Judas who betrayed Jesus, and Peter who denied him the night of his trial.

A very common fruit and popular in New Zealand, the passionfruit does not have much of a profile in other nations: in the United States it is barely known at all. Even in Hawaii, where it could be imagined the passionfruit would fit perfectly into the landscape, it is uncommon, and is called *lilikoi*.

 Paua

An edible univalve shellfish, formally called *Haliotis iris* and first listed by a European in 1773, paua is something of an acquired taste, though one must not be put off by the unusual blackish colouring of the ample flesh, and the vigorous pounding it must be given before cooking. Paua is closely related and similar to the North American abalone, but there is one major difference: although abalone has an attractive shell, next to paua it looks bland.

Paua shell, once polished, displays a miraculous series of opalescent swirls in glowing deep-sea colours, like a technicoloured mother-of-pearl. Maori fishermen used fragments of the shell as lures. In contemporary art circles, the shell is widely used for decorative effects and making designer jewellery.

 Pavlova

It is always dangerous to say when a specific food or cake was invented. Centuries ago someone seems to have discovered the delights of baking egg whites with sugar, in the old Swiss town of Mehr-in-Yghen, now known as Meiringen, hence the word meringue. The French soon added whipped cream and sometimes a pastry base, then called the dessert *vacherin*.

This was ages before the Russian mega-star ballerina Anna Pavlova danced in New Zealand in 1926. Her most famous solo was 'The Dying Swan', for which she wore a filmy white costume of silk and feathers. Someone in New Zealand put together the traditional meringue-and-cream dessert with a new name, pavlova. The first recipe with that name appeared in New Zealand in 1929.

 ## Pedestrian crossing

From the Latin *pes* (foot), pedestrian has been in use since the 18th century, but not concerned with walking — it described someone who was plodding, even boring, in personality.

In *Word Court* linguist Barbara Wallraff points out that, in earlier centuries, there was little need to describe people who walked to their destination because nearly everybody did just that. William Wordsworth is credited with first using an actual word, pedestrian, to designate foot-walkers — in 1791.

Pedestrian crossings came much later, obviously after cars took to the streets. But they're not always called that. Some nations call them crosswalks; in other places they're zebra crossings. To those people, the New Zealand preference for pedestrian crossing seems, well, pedestrian.

 ## Pelorus Jack

This dolphin was one of New Zealand's most famous citizens between 1888 and 1912.

Properly called *Grampus griseus* (a Risso's dolpin), Pelorus Jack liked human company and chose the busy waters between Wellington and Nelson, specifically French Pass, to indulge this predilection. A familiar and regular sight, Jack bustled up alongside all craft, sported and played and showed off. So popular was the dolphin, that in 1904 the New Zealand government passed a protection order for him, thought to be the first act of state in world history especially to protect a sea creature.

He wasn't seen after 1912, and is remembered in a children's song, chocolate fish and a few fragments of grainy turn-of-the-century film footage. The latter raises two interesting points about the validity of his popular name. First, he seldom went to Pelorus Sound, after whom he was named. And second, according to experts who have examined the film, 'he' could very likely have been Pelorus *Jill*.

 Penny dropped

It means to understand suddenly — that a complex or difficult concept has become miraculously clear, that you've remembered a name or face, that you've seen through a swindle. The expression is also an interesting example of linguistic hangover, since New Zealand changed to cents in 1967 and has not used pennies since.

 Petrol

The word is an abbreviation of petroleum (from the mediaeval Latin for oil from stones), a substance that is actually broken down into some half-a-dozen other products besides the one known as petrol.

But petrol is not the only name by which the flammable vehicle fuel is known. Americans determinedly call it gas, even though it is a liquid, and variations such as benzine and gasoline have cropped up during the auto trade's history.

By cultural osmosis, New Zealanders are aware of the alternative terms and even occasionally use them. But conservatism prevails in many areas — car enthusiasts, especially racers, are known as petrol-heads, and when a car is showing close to empty, its driver will head for a petrol station.

Q Phar Lap

One of New Zealand's most famous exports did not sing opera or play rugby or split atoms. And he had four legs. Phar Lap was born near Timaru, and when an Australia-based but New Zealand-born trainer predicted his potential, the horse was taken across the Tasman in 1928. By the time he was five years old he was the greatest stake winner in Australasia and was described as the racing phenomenon of the century. After he made a considerable impact in the United States, his somewhat mysterious death there in 1932 caused mutterings that have never completely died down.

His name was a combination of Sri Lankan words which mean 'lightning moving quickly across the sky'.

Q Pie

What New Zealanders call a pie is not quite the same as what is called just pie in other countries. A New Zealand pie is for individual eating, a one-stop meal. It is a closed pastry case containing any one of a wide variety of fillings — meat, chicken, curry, vegetables or combinations thereof.

Elsewhere, pie more commonly refers to a much larger offering, from which slices are cut for individual people to eat. In New Zealand, to buy a pie does not mean purchasing a large fancy dessert that is intended to be divided among several people. It means to buy a small version for just one person — for lunch, a snack, sustenance during a journey or a sports match.

A one-person version is commonly available in Britain, the pork pie, but this has a surprisingly low profile in New Zealand.

Q Pie cart

This is a long, low-slung caravan which customarily parks (by arrangement) in the same urban street spot each night and serves food out its side windows. The menu inclines towards fast-cooked and filling, rather than elegance, and traditionally includes hot pies (see **Pie**) with various trimmings such as mashed potatoes and peas, plus takeaways of the hamburger type. The term 'pie cart' has been in common urban usage since the 1914–18 war.

Pig Islander

This informal name for a New Zealander, *very* informal (to be honest — in doubtful taste), is believed to be based on the fact that in 1769 Captain Cook introduced New Zealand's first pigs — domestic ones, many of which escaped into the wild, so that an impression somehow grew of a country rich in wild pigs. Hence the early slang description — accepted with tolerant goodwill — of New Zealand itself as the Pig Islands. Gradually the phrase became associated with the people who lived in the nation itself. Sometimes, and perhaps confusingly, the term seems to apply only to either North Islanders or South Islanders.

In 1966 eminent poet James K. Baxter lifted the term into literary respectability by using the title *Pig Island Letters* for a major collection of poems.

Q Pikelet

This word has nothing to do with a fish. A New Zealand pikelet is a small, round, cake-like snack, made from batter which includes leavening, dropped directly onto a hot cooking surface, then turned and cooked on the other side. It looks like a small and fairly thick pancake, and is best eaten within ten minutes of being cooked (with some butter, jam and cream). It is known elsewhere as a drop scone or girdle scone, but New Zealand sticks to the name pikelet (from the original Welsh word *bara-pyglyd*).

Q Piker

To an Englishman, a pike is either a kind of fish, a mediaeval spear-like weapon (pikestaff) or a small hill. The extended noun, piker, can mean a vagrant in Britain but is not often heard (though in Australia a confident trickster is very occasionally referred to as a piker).

An American meaning, which developed about 1930, transferred piker to another kind of person — one who shirks, is timid and ventures little. This is the meaning adopted by New Zealanders, to whom a piker is a person to be scorned because they duck responsibility or leave parties early. Doing so has become a verb, to pike, or, occasionally, to pike out.

Q Pimple

Although still often used in New Zealand, this word is regarded as old-fashioned by those who prefer to use the American equivalent, zit.

Q Plaits

From the Latin *plicare*, to fold, the word is common enough, to describe the system of weaving hair into a three-way column rope. But the word plait can cause some puzzlement to non-New Zealanders, who would always call the same thing a braid.

Q Plonk

This casual term for alcoholic drink, usually wine, was derived by Second World War New Zealand and Australian soldiers from the original French *vin blanc*.

Q Plunket

William Lee Plunket was born in Ireland, son of an archbishop who was also a baron. The young Plunket went into the diplomatic service and was eventually appointed as Governor of New Zealand from 1904 to 1910. His wife was from the highest orders of British society, daughter of the Marquis of Dufferin and Ava. But Lady Victoria Alexandrina Plunket did not rest on her social laurels. She took a great interest in the New Zealand Society for the Promotion of the Health of Women and Children and in 1907 agreed to the society changing its name in her honour.

The Plunket Society was wide-ranging and well organised, with many clinics to which mothers took young babies for weighing, medical checks and advice on diet. Lady Victoria Plunket was instrumental in establishing these branches (known as Plunket rooms), and long after she left New Zealand her name lived on in a succession of terms such as Plunket nurse (specialising in the care of mothers and babies), Plunket baby (babies brought up under the advice of the society's founder Sir Frederic Truby King) and Plunket book (the written record of a baby's growth progress).

One visitor to New Zealand, unfamiliar with the term Plunket room, thought that it meant somewhere to take your baby and plunk it down.

(See also **Karitane**)

Q Plurry

Nineteenth-century Maori liked the sound and impact of the word bloody, but the Maori language has no b, g or l so, by consonant substitution, they came up with plurry, which is used as a similar expletive. Curiously, although the word is now only occasionally used by Maori, Europeans more or less adopted this version back into English as a polite alternative to saying bloody.

(See also **Py korry**)

Q Pohutukawa

This native tree forms one of New Zealand's most noble sights. Maori have long known that juice from the inner bark can help to cure toothache, soothe inflammation and heal wounds.

In 1769, when botanist Joseph Banks first saw *Metrosideros excelsa*, he observed that its comparatively short trunk and many massive arms could be suitable for the crooks and elbows of boat-building. By the mid-19th century pohutukawa timber was being extensively used for the ribs of sailing ships and proved very serviceable in salt water (though kauri timber lasted even longer).

In maturity, pohutukawa is a tree of spectacularly large and often gnarled growth. Found more commonly in the north of the country, it has small bushy flowers, brilliant red, in December, causing it to be known as the New Zealand Christmas tree.

North of Gisborne, in the settlement of Te Araroa, there is a land reserve gifted to the government by the descendants of warrior Rere Kohu, on condition that the pohutukawa tree in the reserve is never touched. The tree in question, the largest pohutukawa in New Zealand (indeed, the largest in the world!), is believed to have started growing in the 1600s or even earlier.

According to traditional belief, the pohutukawa tree at Cape Reinga, the northernmost tip of the North Island, is even older, and may date back a millennium or longer. It is sacred to the Maori, who regard this tree as the departure point for spirits of people who have died, and are leaving this world en route to the other world.

Q Poi

A small ball made of dried bull-rush fluff bound together with long strips of dried leaves and suspended on a short or very long string, the poi is swung by Maori women in very decorative and complex patterns. The spectacular quadruple long poi, where a performer swings two balls in contrary motion with one hand, and the same with the other hand, appears to defy the rules of centrifugal force.

In earlier times the ball was sometimes spelt 'poe' and was used by both genders, especially when Maori men were accustoming their wrists to the strong and swift movements required for battle. In contemporary times the poi is used only by women and is often made of crushed plastic bags with appropriate decoration.

Americans who have visited Hawaii are sometimes confused by the word's meaning in New Zealand since poi in Hawaii is a kind of heavy starch pudding cooked from roots.

'Po karekare ana'

It is probably the best-known piece of music to arise from New Zealand. A love song, it tells of warm feelings travelling across the ripples of lake water (which is how the opening phrase can be translated). The words were first published in 1919 in a little booklet to raise funds for returned Maori soldiers, and described as a 'ditty emanating from North of Auckland'.

Various copyright tangles have existed ever since, starting in 1926 with a declaration that composer Alfred Hill was responsible for the tune. In 1987 the lyrics were posthumously registered as copyright to Paraire Tomoana, who died in 1946. Thus, according to law, the words came into the public domain in 1996.

Maori words :

Po karekare ana
Nga wai o Waiapu
Whitu atu koe, e hine
Marino ana e.
E hine e
Hoki mai ra
Ka mate ahau
I te aroha e.

(Note: The word Waiapu is traditionally replaced by the name of a water area associated with the district from which the singer comes.)

English words :

The rippling waters of (Waiapu)
Break against its banks
But settle into calmness
When my lover crosses.
Oh my beloved!
Come back to me
Without your love
I will surely die.

 ## Poke the borax

In the Australian native dialect of Wathawurung, the word *borak* means no, not or nonsense, and this was adopted by white Australians as a form of put-down. Somewhere along the line it gained the English verb 'to poke', and turned into a plural. But when we poke *borak* or borax we are using an Australian Aboriginal word to make fun of someone.

It has nothing to do with the chemical substance called hydrated disodium tetraborate (otherwise known as borax).

 ## Polynesian

The word is Greek and means many islands. Cartographers and ethnologists agree that Polynesia means that area of the Pacific which includes Hawaii, Samoa, Easter Island, Tonga, New Zealand, Tahiti, Niue, the Cook Islands and Tokelau. And all the indigenous people within that area are called Polynesians. Each group is different from the other — Samoan, Maori, Cook Island — but all are of the Polynesian race.

This causes a minor semantic confusion in New Zealand. The local Polynesian race is called Maori, who can be differentiated from the others by calling the others Pacific Islanders. But over a period, New Zealanders referring to Pacific Islanders seemed to find the phrase too cumbersome and started to substitute the slightly easier Polynesians. This becomes awkward in a statement like Maori and Polynesians, which is a semantic nonsense, since Maori *are* Polynesians. It's like saying Californians and Americans.

Pommy, Pom

Once a very common informal term meaning a person born or raised in the British Isles, its origin has been allocated to various sources. The word has often been described as an acronym of either 'prisoners of Mother England' or 'permit migration Ireland or England'. Other versions have it related to Pompey (naval slang for Portsmouth) or a version of *pommes* (potatoes, eaten by British troops) or a diminutive of pomegranates, a fruit that supposedly shares the rosiness of its cheeks with those of Britishers.

Lexicographer Harry Orsman put paid to all the above theories in his scholarly 1997 examination of the term, in which he describes it as the result of a kind of antipodean rhyming slang. British immigrants became referred to as Jimmy Grants, which in time was replaced by pomegranates, then shorted to pommy and, eventually, pom!

In the second half of the 20th century, a certain distaste for British ways caused 'pommy' to be frequently associated with the word whingeing (complaining) and/or bastard.

Pom and pommy have become somewhat imaginatively extended over the years, so now you sometimes hear Pomland, Pomgolia and sometimes Pongolia — all slang terms for England.

Q Poncy

Originally related to the French and Spanish words for prostitute, poncy has always meant ostentatious or pretentious behaviour, but in Britain also carries a side meaning of involvement as a pimp for ladies of the night. The latter connotation is completely absent in New Zealand, where poncy could be said of the most eminently respectable person — *if* they were showy with money, precious in their manner or snobbish in their associations.

The derivation has nothing to do with the Auckland suburb of Ponsonby.

 Pop

One of the meanings of pop is a short, sharp sound. In New Zealand this has taken on a far wider meaning, usually involving making a movement that is quick and easy. This surfaces very prominently in all forms of household advice, especially cooking where, according to magazines, radio and television, we should pop something into a marinade, pop it under a grill, pop some cheese on top, pop it into a quick oven, pop it through a blender, etc.

Socially, to pop in signifies an informal visit, probably a brief one. To pop over means to visit soon and to pop back means to return later. Telephone receptionists frequently advise that they will pop you through to a desired extension, but don't expect a short, sharp sound: the most likely result will be recorded muzak or robot voicemail. To pop off can mean to leave somewhere fairly abruptly; it can also mean to die.

 Possie

Pronounced 'pozzie', this is an abbreviation of position. To gain a good possie means being placed advantageously — for shooting ducks, watching rugby or setting up a market stall.

 Pottle

A small and insubstantial container, meant to hold a portion of berry fruits, or other foods, sometimes moist, that need to be contained for a short period (such as yoghurt or fruit salad).

(See also **Chip**)

Q Powhiri

A formal Maori welcome, involving careful placing of the hosts on one side of an invisible line, and the visitors (manuhiri) on the other side. Alternating representatives from each side make speeches, and each speech *must* be rounded off with a song, either from the speaker themselves, a stand-in (who is a better singer) or the entire group. When all the speakers and songs reach a conclusion, the visitors advance over the invisible line and are greeted individually (usually with a hongi) by the hosts. The visitors then have a place for their feet on the host's territory.

Q Possum

In 1837 some bright spark had the idea that if opossums from Australia were released in New Zealand, they might multiply — and provide the basis for a fur industry. Multiply they did. Within 100 years opossums in New Zealand outnumbered sheep, far outnumbered people and had started to destroy thousands of young trees and spread cattle diseases. But the fur industry has never really caught up with them: they're an aggressive bunch, their skins are often scarred and the fur colour varies from district to district, making the pelts hard to match. The name is a variant of a native American word for the beast. Some people claim there are two slightly different kinds of animal, one called opossum and the other called simply possum, but the general public doesn't seem aware of this fine distinction and has just slipped into saying possum for everything.

Q The Pot

Although New Zealand has a strong affiliation with the astronomical group known as the Southern Cross, many Kiwis have trouble actually finding it when they look up at the sky. Not so with the Belt of Orion, a bright grouping that stands out in the night sky.

Orion was a hunter from Greek mythology whose many (and often lustful) adventures included being blinded by a vengeful king protecting his princess-daughter, and then flying towards the sun to seek the return of his sight, which the sun granted. Stalled in an attempt to ravish another maiden, Orion was eventually killed by a disturbed scorpion.

Disregarding such legends and their rather slim relationship to the constellation named after him, New Zealanders relentlessly call this star group the Pot, simply because that's what it looks like: a squarish group of bright spots with a 'handle' to one side. It rises in the east every night, tracks across the sky in patterns according to the season and always sets in the west.

Even to the august staff of the Auckland Stardome Observatory the name is accepted as quite valid for the star group, since legends of Orion have little impact on South Pacific life.

Rarely in New Zealand, but sometimes in Australia, it can be called the Saucepan and is not to be confused with a similar American downhome habit of calling Sagittarius the Teapot.

 # Professional

In general terms, the word has two slightly different meanings: a person who is paid for doing a job, rather than doing it for no wages (who would be amateur), or an occupation, the practice of which requires official certification after a period of prescribed academic study (e.g. architect, accountant, doctor, lawyer, dentist). In New Zealand the word has developed a third meaning: good, indicating a perception of quality.

The New Zealand show business award for the Most Professional Performer doesn't mean that the winner earns more than anyone else, but that they do their job better. In May 2000, a senior television executive published a statement that 'TV news now is markedly more professional'. Yet in international terminology it always was professional — TV news has never been done by amateurs. In this context the word meant that its standards had improved (nothing to do with how much those involved were paid).

Pukeko

Properly *Porphyrio melanotus*, the pukeko is a swamp-loving New Zealand bird approximately the size of a full-grown hen, blackish-purple in colour, with an absurd red-lipped beak, long spindly red legs and a jaunty tail that constantly flicks up the white feathers underneath. The pukeko (sometimes known just as a puke, pronounced 'pook') is a common sight, even in cities when roads run near water, but the bird seems safe from human predators.

Although legend persists that it can be made into soup, you never seem to meet anyone who's actually tried it, and its flesh is so hard to cook that the bird is subject to jokes. Possibly this self-confidence that it will never reach a menu gives the bird its endearing quirkiness.

(Folklore recipe: To cook a pukeko, pluck and draw the bird, then place it in a pot together with a stone. Boil gently for some 3 hours — then eat the stone.)

Q Puku

In the Maori language it means a swelling and, by association, a stomach. This latter is its commonest application, particularly when the stomach being referred to is big. But not always — slim people with no waistline problems, even children, can say after a meal that they have a full puku and it doesn't indicate obesity, just that their stomach can't take any more!

Q Py korry

Those of New Zealand's early colonists who were the pious kind must have preferred saying the innocuous by golly (instead of by God, which is what it means). Maori took the phrase into their own language, but couldn't pronounce it accurately, so by golly became py korry.

Although in the 21st century most Maori have become as

proficient in pronouncing English as their own language, py korry is still occasionally heard, often by Maori using it in a jocular way.

(See also **Plurry**)

Q The Queen of New Zealand

New Zealand's Head of State is Elizabeth II, Queen of New Zealand. Her status in relationship to New Zealand has altered several times. At the time she became Queen (February 1952) her status was officially described (in Britain) as 'Elizabeth the Second, by the Grace of God Queen of this Realm and of all her other Realms and Territories, Head of the Commonwealth, Defender of the Faith'. New Zealand was one of the other realms and territories.

A specific change was made a year later in 1953 when a proclamation announced that she would now be titled 'Elizabeth the Second by the Grace of God of the United Kingdom, New Zealand and her other Realms and Territories Queen, Head of the Commonwealth, Defender of the Faith'. This time New Zealand was actually specified.

A further and rather important change came in 1974, when a Royal Titles Act altered the style and title to 'Elizabeth the Second, by the Grace of God Queen of New Zealand and Her other Realms and Territories, Head of the Commonwealth, Defender of the Faith'. No reference at all was made to the United Kingdom.

The significance of this change is that the Queen became New Zealand's head of state quite separately from Britain. She no longer held the crown in New Zealand simply because she was Queen of the United Kingdom, but 'in style and right of New Zealand'. This gives the country itself the status of an independent sovereign realm — a kingdom standing on its own two feet.

If the House of Windsor is ever deposed from office in Britain, under the current law, Elizabeth *remains* Queen of New Zealand regardless.

(See also **Kingdom**)

Queen's Birthday

In 1910 when King George V came to the throne, his birthday was in (British) mid-summer, 3 June. The celebration of his birthday became an established public holiday. The following king, Edward VIII was on the throne for such a short time (he wasn't crowned) that celebrating his birthday didn't become an issue. Edward's brother, King George VI, was born on 14 December, not a good date for a holiday, as it was cold (in Britain) and close to Christmas. A decision was made to revert to the June date and declare this the official royal birthday. George VI's daughter, Elizabeth II, was born on 21 April, but the June date remained.

New Zealand organised its own celebration with the Sovereign's Birthday Observance Act of 1952 which declares a public holiday to celebrate the sovereign's birthday on the first Monday in June.

 Queen Street farmer

Arising during the 1950s, the term denotes a city-living business-person who owns a rural property as a financial proposition but is not a working farmer. It has a distinctly derogatory connotation, when said by either city or country people. Sometimes in the Wellington district, you'll hear it as Featherston Street farmer.

Queue

Possibly because of its early links with Britain, New Zealand favours the word queue to describe a group of people waiting for something and standing behind one another in a row while doing so.

The word originates in the Latin *cauda*, meaning tail. The word travelled through the French language, becoming *queue*, then into English, where it has been since the 16th century. Then it still meant tail, even in English: by the 18th century it was being used to describe the little pigtail then fashionable at the back of gentlemen's wigs.

But bigger cities, wars and shortages caused people to have to wait for goods and services, and the word queue moved from being a pigtail to being a row of people — at least in Britain and New Zealand. Canada and the United States adopted the alternative expression 'in line'. If you say queue to Americans they think you're talking about playing billiards.

R

Q Raddle

In rural areas, raddle is a common term describing a heavy piece of coloured chalk (as thick as a banana) used to mark livestock for identification assistance when drafting.

The word began its life in very old English as *rudd*, meaning red. For centuries farmers needed to use a kind of temporary scourable mark on livestock, especially sheep. The one commonly used was made from a red ochre and by the 16th century this was called ruddle because of its colour. Later, variant pronunciations of the word began to be used: reddle or raddle.

Several descendants of those uses are still with us. The old *rudd* survives in the word ruddy, meaning a healthy reddish complexion from having an outdoor life. And you'll still hear raddled, which really means painted, as in women wearing too much obvious make-up, especially rouge, which is red. (Raddled is often also heard meaning tough, wrinkled, ugly, well-used, although in dictionary terms is still means painted red.)

New Zealand has stuck to the pronunciation *raddle* for marking sheep, although for many years now a variety of colours has been used and they may come in a spray can rather than chalk form.

Q Rapt

Meaning totally engrossed, from the Latin *rapere*, to seize, the word was out of fashion for many decades because of its rather poetic image. But in recent times has been taken up by young New Zealanders as a synonym for stoked or chuffed.

Q Real estate

The word real comes ultimately from the Latin *res*, meaning thing. Thus its various modern meanings are to do with truth — things that exist or occur in the physical world. It often occurs as a qualifier, referring to value measured in terms of actual price, income or purchasing power, as opposed to nominal, sentimental or cultural value (e.g. the real value of greenstone on the international jade market).

Real estate generally means property that is immovable — it is land, it exists, it can't be carried away. A shade of the meaning can be found in some wills, where you could have a fortune in shares and trusts and insurance policies, but in legal terms those parts of your estate will be described separately from anything solid, such as land and properties, which can't be carried or transported. That is described as real. Hence, real estate.

The United States favours the terms realty and realtor, which have the same origin and meaning.

Q Rellies

It's the word relatives abbreviated to the baby-talk, rellies. This affectation, officially called a hypocorism, is in wide use in New Zealand: as in cardies, pressies, drinkies, kiddies, Chrissy, hostie, brickie, flattie, sammie, sickie, yachtie, etc. (Hypocorism means endearing, euphemistic or child-like terminology.)

Q Reserve

An area of publicly owned land that is set aside for recreation, usually (but not necessarily) in an urban surrounding. There is no set size for a reserve — it may be large enough to contain sports facilities, or just a small grassy area. Reserves may also be designated for a specific purpose, e.g. a scenic reserve.

(See also **Domain**)

Right as rain

Meaning that everything is in an excellent state, in good condition and happy, right as rain is closely related to the British expressions 'right as a trivet' and 'right as ninepence'. New Zealand, however, seems to prefer alliterative expressions, especially if they have any bearing on the local landscape — and in an agricultural country, rain is more important than trivets or ninepence.

(See also **Good as gold**)

 Ring up

It means to make a phone call. Scotsman Alexander Graham Bell (who went to work in the United States) patented the first telephone in 1876. A major communications firm turned down the instrument, which they dismissed as 'an interesting novelty with no commercial possibilities'. Later, the phone patent became one of the most valuable in world history.

In New Zealand, early use of the phone system involved vigorously turning a handle which made one long ring to alert an operator at a central exchange. Alternatively the handle was turned in a combination of short and long in a code that alerted whoever else was sharing the party line that they should answer. This led to the rise of the phrases to ring someone (up) or to give them a ring.

Although individual phone lines and button dials and electronic chirpers have replaced actual bells, the expression is still widely used.

Q Roaring Meg

While a legend persists that one particular young 19th-century woman made a lot of noise and fuss crossing one particular New Zealand river (a tributary of the Kawarau near Cromwell), her story is echoed by legends of several other noisy women. And the ladies must have got about some: there are Roaring Megs in four separate parts of New Zealand, as well as in Scotland, Ireland, England and Australia. Perhaps it's not a true New Zealand legend after all.

 Rogernomics

Like Thatcherism or, more appropriately, Reaganomics, the term Rogernomics is a simple play on the name of a politician, Sir Roger Douglas, New Zealand's Minister of Finance from 1984 to 1988. Douglas reduced direct taxation but also introduced a new goods and services tax. He also removed certain sectors of the economy from state control (e.g. postal services and air and rail travel). Rogernomics was first noticed in print in 1985 and was rapidly accepted as a standard description for that period of fiscal history.

 Rooster

Obviously rooster means the male of a domestic hen. But there is another application in New Zealand to describe men (never women) who are either slightly more sure of themselves than is pleasant — perhaps cocksure, cocky (which is the connection with roosters) — or are held in faint derision. In both cases, a rooster is dismissed as a person who is faintly ridiculous — at least in the eyes of one beholder.

 Ropeable

Although derived (obviously) from rope, New Zealanders usually use the word ropeable to mean very angry indeed — almost requiring restraint, fit to be tied. And that usage does not commonly occur elsewhere (except perhaps Australia).

Q Rubber

Universally, rubber means the bouncy or stretchy substance resulting from dried plant latex. New Zealanders use the word in all its normal extended meanings, such as a division of a bridge game, a cheque that isn't honoured, a thin band used to hold a roll of papers, a printing stamp, a person who gapes inquisitively (a rubbernecker) and so on.

But one customary use in New Zealand sometimes requires explanation: a rubber is the word usually used to describe a pencil eraser. Other countries, such as Australia and the United States, customarily call this an eraser and retain rubber as a euphemism for condom.

Q Rubbish

Unwanted useless matter discarded as waste, rubbish can involve practical substances such as the leftovers from industry or households, or less practical things like stupid talk, endless bureaucracy or pointless ritual. Elsewhere the words trash or garbage are commonly used for these things, and although New Zealanders would understand those words, they tend to continue saying rubbish.

To a New Zealander the term rubbish tin is self explanatory. Other people might call it a trash can or garbage bin. It can be big enough to hold all waste from a household or a building, or as small as the independent lift-top container called a kitchen tidy.

S

 Sandshoes

The American term trainers has some currency in New Zealand, but the British name for the same thing — plimsolls — has never caught on. New Zealanders frequently call them sandshoes.

A sandshoe, made of canvas (usually white) with a rubber sole, and sometimes called a tennis shoe, is marginally different from elaborate trainers, which are sometimes ankle high, with swooping heels, huge air-pocket soles and netting inserts. To a population orientated towards beaches, sandshoes were initially considered ideal for just one thing — wearing on a beach (if shoes were worn at all there) and absolutely unacceptable in any semi-formal context.

The growth in popularity of American-influenced sandshoes began with a moderate inroad of the term 'running shoes' and later elaborate trainers gave that kind of shoe a far wider social acceptance, partly because their impressive cost warranted them some respect as wardrobe items, and partly because, the bigger and more decorated they became, the more they were regarded as real shoes.

But, for the beach, New Zealanders tend towards the simpler, lighter, less spectacular sandshoes.

Sausages

This seems simple enough, but the word has slightly different applications depending on where you are. In some places overseas, a sausage is a large item from which slices are cut, while the smaller domestic variety — of which any New Zealander can eat three or four — are known in some countries as links, presumably because they're joined together in a string. In New Zealand the word sausage does for both — those linked in a string and those from which chunks are cut. Very small ones have a different name altogether.

Snags, snarlers and bangers are all words for sausages. Snags derives from the Lancashire snackles, meaning small morsels of food. Snarlers originated in the military, when some armed forces thought the noise of frying sausages sounded like dogs snarling. Other armed forces heeded the popping sound of them frying, hence called them bangers.

(See also **Cheerios**)

 ## Savouries

Savouries are small, non-sweet snack items, sometimes quite elaborate, which are served not as a meal, but as an accompaniment to socialising. Other places call them hors d'oeuvres or canapés.

(See also **Nibbles**)

 ## Say a few words

Carl V. Smith's classic 1947 book *From N to Z* says: 'Next to watching a football match, a horse race, or criticising the Government, there is nothing a New Zealander likes more than making a speech. This is fulfilment of an unwritten law in New Zealand that everybody should be given an opportunity to improve his oratory.'

Certainly if European New Zealanders have contributed little else to local cultural ritual, they certainly have embraced The Speech. It is often the only ritual performed on notable occasions, in spite of the fact that most people hate listening to them and few people are any good at making them.

Referring to a speech as 'saying a few words' somehow panders to the recognition of this boredom — it apologetically suggests that although you have to listen, it will be short. This is often not true: the few words can extend to 30 minutes or more.

Q Scarfie

The University of Otago in the city of Dunedin inspires a specially strong loyalty among its students. As is normal worldwide, the university logo and colours appear in various manifestations on appropriate garments, including the scarf.

By New Zealand standards, Dunedin winters are cold and woollen scarves a necessity. But the students' affection for their scarves meant that scarves of some kind were worn nearly all year, whether in university colours or not. Hence, the term scarfie, meaning a university student.

The expression is fairly regional in use and might be greeted with incomprehension outside Dunedin, though the movie *Scarfies*, concerning the misadventures of a group of Dunedin students, did a great deal to widen national understanding of the word.

Q Scone

Small lightweight dough-cakes cooked in an oven or sometimes on a griddle, scones often contain cheese, dates or raisins but nothing too sweet. Scones tend to be held in derision by people who are either unable themselves to make them, or have only ever bought them in a shop — which is not wise. To be excellent, scones have to be freshly home-made — there's nothing better.

The word scone is derived from the German *schonbrot* (fine bread) and is pronounced various ways. New Zealanders settle for *sconn*. Scone also appears in New Zealand with another meaning and from another source: the old British word *sconce*, referring to the head. Reduced to scone, it has little or no connection with baked cakes except for sounding the same. This scone turns up in head expressions: to use your scone (think carefully), to be off your scone (functioning abnormally) or to do your scone (express marked anger). Americans seldom refer to scones, but if they do, they call them baking powder biscuits.

Q Scoria

This word, which refers to small chunks of lava-flow rock, used in building, concreting and road surfacing, is found elsewhere but is much more widely used in New Zealand.

Q Scroggin

This is a self-made and easily carried snack food favoured by trampers and bushwalkers. Sometimes known as trail mix, it consists of portions of high-energy items mixed together, which can be dipped into when a sugar rush will help the day's activities. The name is thought to have arisen from the initial letters of the traditional ingredients: sultanas, chocolate, raisins, orange peel (candied), ginger (crystallised), glucose barley sugar, imagination and nuts.

Wide variation exists within those guidelines. Different kinds of nuts turn up in scroggin, depending on what's available: cashews, macadamias, almonds, peanuts and, to stretch the word nuts a bit, pumpkin or sunflower seeds and sesame lumps.

Whatever form the chocolate takes, it must be of the melt-in-the-mouth kind, not melt-in-the-pocket. Imagination can include dried banana chips, dried apricots, prunes, little rice crackers, jellybeans etc.

Scroggin can be made into individual carry-bags, or one large communal supply. In the latter case, etiquette requires that each person taking a helping of scroggin must take from the mix in general and not just pick out their favourite bits.

Q Scrub

There are several meanings for scrub. Once it was a slang term for a contemptible person, invariably male. Because of this, the word has often been used as a synonym for shrub, thus gaining a slight meaning of something unimpressive in size and stunted (compared with a tree). New Zealand vernacular often refers to scrub-cutting, meaning shrub-like growth that is not respected enough to keep.

Late in the 19th century the term began to be used by university students when referring to an athlete who was not good enough to make the representative team: his name had been scrubbed off the list of those considered the cream of the college's athletes. He was a scrub.

In recent times the term has re-emerged, mainly as American slang, but with somewhat the same meaning as before: a contemptible (male) person, or someone about whom the speaker had reason to feel aggrieved.

(The expression scrub is not really related to the more common term scrubber, who is invariably female. Scrubber is an old military term for a lowly woman, and often one whose morals were loose. The word use may have arisen through the fact that women needing employment scrubbed floors, or it may have carried the connotation of someone being very poor and unkempt, who scrubbed and scraped a living together.)

Q Section

The Latin word *sectio* was applied to things that were cut and survives in words like vivisection or dissection. Within this verbal framework, the real estate term 'section' means a piece of land cut off from a greater piece, or each piece of a considerable division.

In New Zealand the word commonly describes the piece of land on which a house is situated, but the term is not necessarily universal. Americans seldom use it, instead usually describing their own piece of domestic land as the yard, and what a New Zealander would describe as an empty section is a vacant lot.

Shagroon

This word is not widely heard in New Zealand nowadays, but was fairly common in olden times, when European settlers were coming to live here in the 19th century.

Shagroon is possibly descended from Gaelic *seachran* (pronounced *shaugran*) meaning wanderer and the English version has been spelt various ways. When used in New Zealand it meant settlers coming to New Zealand and occurred principally in the Canterbury area. Its especial reference was when referring (in a derogatory way) to settlers from Australia who were considered stragglers and were not immigrants belonging to the Canterbury Association, who were thought of as being from a more elevated class.

In the late 20th century (since 1997, to be exact) musician brothers Mike and Phil Garland have revived the lost word shagroon as the name for their Canterbury-based band. Known also as Bush Telegraph, they were looking for a name that sounded right when they were playing engagements in the Irish/Celtic genre but which had a distinctive New Zealand flavour. Shagroon was perfect.

 Shaky Isles

This somewhat scornful description, usually said by Australians, refers to the fact that New Zealand is reputed to have a great many earthquakes. Australia actually has more earthquakes than New Zealand, but often in sparsely inhabited areas, so they are not noticed by the population at large. (New Zealand feels between 150 and 200 tremors per year.)

 Sharemilker

A sharemilker works on a dairy farm but not just as an employee — by agreement with the farm-owner, in return for labour and involvement the sharemilker receives a proportion of the farm's

191

income. There are many variations on this: for instance, the farmer may not necessarily own the cows on his or her land, they being the property of the sharemilker, so again an agreement is reached about earnings in relation to input. Besides the sale of milk, there can be subsidiary details regarding the allocation of price received from sale of calves and other livestock.

A similar system in France is called *métayage* and in the United States the word share-cropping relates to the labour of those who harvest the crop for the owner of the land.

The term sharemilker has been common in New Zealand since the early 1900s and the practice has contributed greatly to the strength of the New Zealand dairy industry.

Q Sheila

Sheila has been used in New Zealand since approximately 1900.

Originally the use of the word was somewhat disrespectful — a young woman to whom one was not married. When in love with, or married to a woman, she would not normally be referred to as just 'a sheila' but more often as 'my sheila' or 'the old sheila,' meaning partner or wife.

Sheila is now often heard in a user-friendly context, as a feminine equivalent of bloke. A book surveying strong women in New Zealand history is even called *Stroppy Sheilas* (and the author is a woman).

Q She'll be right

'She' is often used for concepts with no noticeable feminine traits, particularly in the abstract. 'She' can be the current situation, the weather, a vehicle, a tree — anything.

In 'she'll be right' the 'she' is a shorthand way of referring to the project in hand, the problem we're facing or even the world at large. To decree that she'll be right indicates that all those things will have a happy outcome (though sometimes the expression is interpreted as displaying an unrealistic overconfidence).

An American Rotary scholar on exchange in New Zealand for a year became the source of legend when she misunderstood the frequently heard statement 'she'll be right' as a local philosophy of optimism expounded by a New Zealander she assumed was called Shelby Wright.

 Shift

It's what people do when they leave one house, take all their belongings and go to live in another. Move house is understood, but shift house is more generally used.

 Shonky

Shonniker is a Yiddish word for a peddlar. Used by non-Jewish people, the word became corrupted into an offensive term for any Jew — a *Shoniker*: it indicated that a person was shady, untrustworthy and unreliable. Gradually it was abbreviated again to shonky.

To speakers of English, the word had a weird logic, even if they had no idea of its Yiddish origins and insulting connotations. This was because, aurally, it seemed to combine shoddy and wonky. Wonky comes from an old dialect word *wankle*, meaning precarious in health, sickly. But when you say something is shonky, you're using a Yiddish word.

 Shorts

There can't be much doubt that the word shorts came into usage as an abbreviation for short pants. Strangely, the United States stuck to the longer version, and when American men do wear shorts (which is not nearly as frequently as New Zealanders do), they're customarily referred to in full as short pants. For

Americans, shorts usually means underpants.

The word shorts is also sometimes used to describe the bits and pieces that used to be shown in a cinema before the interval and the main feature: promos, commercials and trailers.

There are variations on the shorts you wear, too. Big baggy ones are called Bombay bloomers, elastic-waisted lightweights are known as boxers and semi-formal ones, made of heavy fabric and worn with knee-length socks, are known as walk shorts.

 Shout

In the sense of paying for someone else, shout is believed to be an old form of the word shot, which meant charge or payment, and in old-time England there was a phrase 'to stand shot', which meant to pay the bill.

But side by side with that is the fact that the bar at English inns tends to be as noisy as any other form of public drinking place, so the phrase 'to shout' came to mean actually yelling at a waiter or bartender, in order to be heard.

Certainly this circumstance applied to the early days of Australian gold-digging, when outback men who had a strike, shared beers with their mates. The crowd in a bar tended to be noisy and boisterous, and for a drinks order to be heard, the man treating his friends literally had to shout his order. Gradually the action of shouting became identified with the object of the exercise.

The term seems to be unknown in the United States, where someone buying drinks or a meal for someone else, is said to be hosting or treating them.

 Shyack

It originates in the Cockney word *chiack* meaning a type of teasing banter — more verbal than physical. In New Zealand the word is far more often used when referring to high-spirited youths (usually male) involved in active but not destructive horseplay.

Q Silver beet

Other places call this rich green vegetable by other names: spinach beet or Swiss chard. Although the dark curly leaves are green, the central stalk is very prominent, very wide and silvery-white. This is believed to be why the plant has been called silver beet in New Zealand since the beginning of the 20th century.

Q Silver fern

Long before the kiwi became an informal national symbol of New Zealand, the beautiful silver fern was a common emblem of the country (which in early times was sometimes referred to as Fernland) and of New Zealanders overseas. The 'Native Rugby Team' that visited Britain in 1888 used it as an emblem and the 1905 All Blacks wore it on their uniforms. Starting in 1900 New Zealand exports featured it on meat and dairy produce. Servicemen during the First World War were commonly known or Fernleaves and in the Second World War they became Silver Ferns.

Since 1956 the official New Zealand coat of arms has discreetly featured the fern and in 1972 the new Auckland–Wellington railcars were called Silver Ferns (because of their shining steel finish). In 1990, a competition was held to find a name for New Zealand's representative netball team: the executive chose the Silver Ferns and the national players have been known by this name ever since. The New Zealand Rugby Football Union has copyrighted the particular shape of the silver frond that is used as the All Black symbol.

Q Singlet

The word singlet, meaning a usually sleeveless vest, is virtually unknown in the United States where the more cumbersome undershirt, undervest or just vest is much more common. When a fashion developed for wearing coloured versions of what were known elsewhere as athletic singlets, Americans called them tank tops. A singlet made of black wool, often worn by New Zealand workmen, is commonly called a bush singlet.

 ## Skerrick

This is one of dozens of words in English which mean a small amount. It originated somewhere in Britain as a fairly uncommon dialect word, used to refer to a halfpenny, a form of money long gone from common usage. A halfpenny was of very small value, so skerrick came to mean anything small, unimportant and hardly noticeable. The word itself has almost vanished in Britain, but still surfaces around New Zealand and Australia, meaning a smidgeon, a tad, a *soupçon*.

 ## Skite

Skite is a very common term in New Zealand, but is actually a shortened version of an old British word. The full original term was blatherskite: blather comes from an Old Norse word *blathra*, meaning nonsense, and skite seems to be interchangeable with skate in some dialects of Northern England and Scotland, meaning a talkative silly person. So a blatherskite was a noisy person who talked a lot of nonsense.

In recent years, Australians and New Zealanders have shortened the word to just skite, and slightly changed its application so that it means someone who irritates people by boasting or bragging unnecessarily.

 ## Slippers

Soft shoes for wearing inside the house, these are never referred to as mules (as in the United States) and are not to be confused with jandals (which in some places, such as Honolulu, are called slippers — causing confusion to New Zealanders when they see a sign outside a restaurant proclaiming 'No jeans, no slippers').

 Smoko

In the days before cigarettes were dubbed dangerous, workers looked forward to regular breaks when they could have a smoke. To mark the beginning of such a rest period, 'smoke ho' or 'smoke oh' was often yelled out. Thus, smoke ho came to mean a work-break and has been used since the first half of the 19th century (the word was first seen in print in 1863).

By 1900 the term had become abbreviated to smoko and this alternated with the rather more formalised smoke-ho until the 1940s when the former word took over and became the norm. Even in situations that do not involve manual labour and where nobody is a smoker, a smoko can be declared, meaning a rest.

Solicitor

In New Zealand this means lawyer and, without fail, members of the public go to them, rather than the other way around. Some other countries call lawyers attorneys and use solicitor in its original sense of someone who is asking you for something.

American airports have announcements alerting waiting passengers that solicitors are not encouraged and need not be paid. They mean con men, prostitutes and beggars, not lawyers.

Q Sounds

A deep bay or inlet of the sea, or a relatively narrow channel between an island and the mainland or between two larger areas of ocean. In New Zealand the term is more widely used than the similar term fiord.

(See also **Fiord**)

Q Spa bath

A non-standard, usually plastic bath, often oval shaped and generous in size, with plumbing so arranged that jets of water play inside the bath area causing bubbles and gentle pressure on the body (or bodies) therein. The name is believed to be an acronym of the Latin phrase *Sanus per aqua*, health through water. A spa bath is usually indoors, as part of a motel or a luxury house.

A spa pool is slightly different, being a small swimming pool structure filled with heated water with some sort of device to bubble the water. Normally it will accommodate several people and is usually installed in an outdoor setting. These bubbling baths and pools are very common in the United States but there both types are called a hot tub or jacuzzi.

Q Sparkling wine

In the early 1980s, the French makers of champagne initiated a court case in New Zealand and effectively prevented any further use of the word champagne to describe bottle-fermented bubbly wine made here.

There is nothing to stop anyone making such wines by exactly the same method as in the Champagne district of France, but caution prevails over how it is described on the label. Hence the coining of descriptions such as champenoise or methode traditionelle, or bottle-fermented or sparkling wine. All three descriptions tend to surprise visitors.

New Zealand firm Hunter's Wines found the ideal solution: their festive wine is called Mirumiru, which is the Maori word for bubbles. But, by a curious irony, the wine is such a successful export that it is seldom seen in New Zealand!

Spit the dummy

The rubber teat commonly given to very young babies to suck is described by Americans and Canadians as a pacifier, whereas New Zealanders retain the British term dummy.

In New Zealand and Australia, the expression 'to spit the dummy' has evolved as a way of describing someone (usually an adult) who has tired of restrictions, or is at loggerheads with some authority and eventually breaks out against them. Sometimes the expression is faintly pejorative, with a connotation that the person concerned is possibly being a bit querulous and railing against an authority that might not deserve the attack.

But everyone knows that when a real baby spits out a real dummy, it is because they intend to make a strident and unwelcome noise.

Spot

To describe an alcoholic drink, this use of spot has developed from the word meaning of 'a small amount', since to have a spot indicates just a few drinks, maybe between one place and the next, or during a brief social meeting, rather than a prolonged drinking session.

Spousal maintenance

This is the official New Zealand term for what other nations call alimony, a word derived from the Latin *alimonia*, meaning sustenance (as in alimentary canal). The pervading image of both terms is that one partner, who is earning, must provide for the one who has become dependent.

Q Spud

The word potato is derived from *batata* in the obscure Taino language of South America. Not everyone uses the word: the French call them apples of the earth and Germans enjoy their *Kartoffel*. But whatever they're called they all need to be dug. The old-time British used a digging instrument called a *spuddle* or *spudder* and eventually the name of the instrument carried over to refer to the things that were being dug up — spuds.

(Contrary to rumour, spud is not an abbreviation of Society for the Prevention of Unhealthy Diets.)

Q Stand

There are four fairly localised uses of the word stand in New Zealand:

(1) With the inexplicable resistance that New Zealanders often display concerning 'gentle' words, a group of trees in this country is seldom called a wood, and never called a copse, coppice or spinney. It is known simply as a stand.

(2) Often abbreviated from grandstand, the stand is where spectators watch horseracing, rugby, cricket etc. — while sitting!

(3) When New Zealanders aim for a political position they stand for election, while Americans run for office. Stand is a slightly eccentric word to use in this context: anyone knows that an election candidate must work hard, moving around to convince people how to cast their votes. The American term seems rather more appropriate, but perhaps New Zealanders find 'run' sounds too eager.

(4) Another common New Zealand use of stand can cause possible confusion to urban visitors. When pedigree animals (especially horses) are said to stand at a certain address, this does not mean they are just standing there — it means that they are available for stud duties, at a fee.

Q State houses

In 1935 New Zealand's first Labour government set up a Department of Housing to assist those who had been left in grim conditions following the major financial depression of a few years before. Many were homeless, and in an effort to avoid slums becoming the norm, the government set out to encourage the provision of a home as a right of citizenship.

Work started on the government-funded project. By 1950 there were over 23,000 state houses, each of simple but practical and well-equipped design, owned by the government, which charged a modest rental to deserving tenants.

Eventually there was a growing change of attitude: increasing numbers of Kiwis wanted to own their own homes and there was some resistance from taxpayers about meeting a growing bill for the ever-burgeoning number of state houses. The government began to offer state houses for sale to their tenants, and government loans became available for private house building.

Q Station

Originating with the Latin word for stand, many meanings have developed around the word station. In general these relate to the site or area where people are based and apparatus is set up for a particular purpose (e.g. military, broadcasting, trains, even restaurant staff).

Since earliest colonial days, New Zealanders applied the above meaning to include big — very big — farms. In Australia and New Zealand there are many farms which are larger than entire European countries (Monaco is only the size of Hagley Park in Christchurch or Cornwall Park in Auckland), and those are the ones referred to as stations. Americans would probably say ranch and in Britain the word estate comes close.

Q Stirrer

Since the ninth century, the word shit has been in (often unacceptable) use, meaning excrement. It developed various other shades of meaning, and by the start of the 20th century it could be used to mean trouble or unpleasantness.

Thus arose the term shit-stirrer, referring to a person who deliberately created trouble. Obviously there were times and places when this term could not be used, so some more polite versions developed, such as stick-stirrer and brown-handled stirrer (though strictly it was not the handle that was brown).

When a person of such prominence as a prime minister used it publicly (Sir Robert Muldoon, who was in the top job from 1975 to 1984), he could reduce it to just stirrer, and everyone knew what he meant.

Q Stock

The word is derived from the Old English *stocc*, the stump of a tree, so it means something solid and dependable. Its several New Zealand meanings include the total goods held within a business, for instance a shop, and the animals on a farm. Hence, stockyards and stock sale, which are to do with animal sales and not with shares. The American use of stock, where most New Zealanders would say shares, can be a little confusing, especially since holding stock in New Zealand tends to mean owning the entire amount rather than a portion, which would be called holding shares.

Q Stoked

Stoke means to add fuel to and tend a fire or furnace. In an era of mainly non-fired energy and when domestic fireplaces are actually illegal in some parts of New Zealand, there is not a great deal of actual stoking going on. But paradoxically, as the actual action of stoking fires became rarer, the word stoked grew in popularity from the 1950s onwards to signify that, like a fire newly charged with fuel, a person is somehow energised, happy, surprised, cheerful, in some way fired up.

Stoked and choked sometimes but rarely, overlap, in that a person who is choked might be stoked with anger. But both words tend to mean happily excited.

'Stoker' had a brief usage during the First World War, to refer to men who had not enlisted in the armed services and were staying home to stoke the fires, but this use is no longer heard.

 ## Stones

They form the middle part of much New Zealand fruit. Any seed that is woody-textured and can't be crunched between the teeth, is a stone. This confuses Americans, who call their fruit stones pits (which confuses New Zealanders, for whom a pit is a hole with nothing in it, rather than a lump of very solid substance). Smaller seeds that can be crunched between teeth and eaten as part of the package, are pips or just seeds.

 ## Stonkered

In the game of marbles, an ancient British dialect word *stonk* was the stake a player must hazard before playing the game (and, he hoped, winning back his stonk). From this there developed a verb 'to be stonkered', with the meaning of being beaten, stymied or exhausted (possibly somehow combined or confused with the nautical term scuppered — ruined).

The term became popular among New Zealand military and after the 1940s the single word, stonkered, went into wide use in New Zealand generally. It can be used within the meanings above — being rendered useless — but with a few variations such as relating to degrees of drunkenness (a bit stonkered), surfeited with food, outwitted, coping with a tricky problem, ruined, tired or even dead!

Q Stoush

In *West Side Story* they called it a rumble. New Zealanders might also sometimes say a barney. But all Kiwis understand stoush — usually a fist-fight or at least a physical confrontation. Stoush is related to the old British word stashie, meaning a quarrel or an uproar. Early settlers to Australia and New Zealand brought the word with them, though in those days the normal spelling was stouch. Early in the 20th century the Aussies and Kiwis had modified the pronunciation into stoush and the original word had become very rare in Britain.

Now we find it as a verb (to stoush, to get stoushed) and as various nouns — a stousher or stoush artist (an enthusiastic fighter) or a neighbourhood stoush. Over the years the meaning has softened a little, so that now a phrase like 'a bit of stoush during the council meeting' does not mean they attacked each other, but just had a vigorous argument.

Q Straight away

It simply means immediately.

Q Strewth

Many words modify the names of God and Jesus into something less offensive (e.g. golly, gosh, gee, crikey etc.). Strewth, too, originates in an expression that mentions the deity: 'in God's truth', said as an exclamation of surprise, wonder or disbelief. Gradually, by the 1800s, the three words became compressed into one.

The word is so deeply ingrained in the New Zealand vocabulary, that the story is often told of a famous New Zealand soprano appearing in a major opera at a world-renowned venue, singing a performance in the English language. At one point she forgot the exact wording of the next spoken line required of her but, recalling that it was meant to express surprise and disbelief, she spoke the first expression of surprise that came to her mind. 'Strewth!' exclaimed the lady elegantly, somewhat to the dismay of her very British colleagues. Fortunately the opera was a comedy.

Q Stroppy

If a person has strong ideas and effective ways of accomplishing their own way of doing things, they can be described as authoritative, or stroppy, depending on your point of view.

The word has been in popular use only since the middle of the 20th century, and is believed to be a mangled abbreviation of 'obstreperous' (noisy, rough, rebellious, resisting control, from the Latin *strepere*, to roar).

A possible influence on the growth of popularity of the word stroppy, could be that around the same time as the word moved into use, many men shaved with a razor which was sharpened daily on a 'strop' — an fairly unyielding strong strip of hard leather.

Q Stubbies

(1) Short thick bottles, usually containing beer.
(2) Outdoor cotton shorts for men.
(See also **Tinny, Tube, Shorts**)

Q Super

A common abbreviation for New Zealand superannuation, which refers to the small weekly payment that has been made to all people over a certain age by the government since 1898. (The New Zealand government was the first in the world to do so.) This used to be called the old age pension, but this was later softened into a benefit, then further gentrified into guaranteed retirement income. Another change of title made it New Zealand super-annuation, commonly called just the super.

But, in a rural context, the word super is also a commonly used abbreviation for superphosphate fertiliser, as spread on farmland. The context should highlight which super is meant — putting a load of super on the back paddock does not mean that granny's pension is being thrown all over the grass.

 Superette

In an attempt to make terms like corner store, dairy or general store rather more upmarket, some such shops call themselves a superette. The super bit (from Latin *supra*, meaning superior and excelling) is intended to mean large, as in supermarket, while -ette (from French) means small (as in cigarette, kitchenette). Thus we have a charming contradiction in terms, an oxymoron: superette indicates a market that is 'big-small'. Nobody in New Zealand cares about the contradiction.

 Swanndri

Officially called a bush shirt, the swanndri is as much a New Zealand icon garment as is the Drizabone in Australia.

It is a company trademark, dating from 1913. Although it was originally spelt Swanndri (which was believed to have been a mistake at the time), the symbol incorporated a swan. The name was based fairly obviously on swan + dry, with the simple connotation that water runs off swans' feathers and doesn't penetrate. The trademark applied to a knee-length outdoor garment, sometimes hooded, loose-fitting and of fabric that was fairly impervious to rain and general forest wetness.

Since the 1940s, the immense popularity of the garments has resulted in their fairly large-scale manufacture. The swanndri has been through various changes of detail — shorter, longer, plain fabric, checked fabric, zipped — but it is still recognisable as a swanndri, though its name is occasionally simplified to just swannie.

Q Swiftie

The meaning of swift is well known (to move quickly, derived from the Old Norse *svifa*, to rove) and besides birds, vehicles, planes and political ideals, all of which move fast, by the start of the 20th century it had developed a pejorative shade of meaning in the word swiftie.

This may have begun in the Navy where a slow-moving rating was ironically described as a swiftie. But a connotation of being tricky and deceitful became attached to the word and by the 1950s Australians were referring to 'pulling a swiftie', meaning that a sharp character had deceived someone, with untruthful facts concerning affairs of the heart or money transactions.

The term is familiar in New Zealand, often applied to organisations at a very high level, e.g. banks inaugurating services that remain free for a pre-determined time then are later charged for, or politicians making certain promises before election then delivering something quite different.

The term is also very familiar in the United States, where a prominent show-business personality is known as Swifty because of the hard bargaining and advantageous deals he is reputed to arrange on behalf of clients.

(But a swifty is not to be confused with a quickie, which is quite different, being a hurried sexual congress without preamble or afterglow.)

Q Swordfish

Genuine swordfish are rare in New Zealand waters. They breed in the Mediterranean and only very occasionally venture this far south. (One genuine broadtail swordfish that did venture towards New Zealand, lived — or rather died — to regret it. All 4 metres of it can be seen in the Auckland Museum.)

But marlin have a sword as well, so the slightly more glamorous word swordfish was sometimes been used to describe them — with resultant minor confusion. The first swordfish caught in New

Zealand waters was by a Major Campbell in 1815, but we'll never know if it actually was a real swordfish, or a marlin.

It certainly impressed people and sparked an interest in fishing of this kind, which survives to this day. But in modern times, you'll be more likely to hear the accurate term marlin used to describe a lucky fisherman's catch.

T

Q Ta

This abbreviation for thank you, in use since the 18th century in Britain and designated as baby-talk, is quite commonly used informally by adult New Zealanders.

Q TAB

It stands for the Totalisator Agency Board. The New Zealand Gaming Amendment Act was passed in 1949 and became law the following year. It was, in part, the outcome of a 1946 Royal Commission into Gaming which recommended that off-course betting on horseracing could somehow be legalised (instead of being handled by illegal bookmakers).

The new act allowed the TAB to have cash investment, postal instructions accompanied by cash, or telephone bets drawing on a deposit already established, or withdrawing from winnings already held in an investor's account. No radio was permitted to operate on TAB premises, no credit was to be permitted and there was to be no seating. The first TAB started operation in March 1951 at Feilding and Dannevirke.

Quite quickly, the initials came to signify not the controlling board, but the various suburban offices at which bets could be placed. Over time, the TAB's activities have widened past horse-racing to accept betting on almost any form of mainstream sport, national and international. And conditions in the suburban outlets have eased up quite a lot since the whole practice started. Some trendy ones are even attached to bars and known as Race Places.

Q Takahe

Properly known as a gallinule, the takahe (*Notornis mantelli*) is a flightless tussock-dwelling bird. It is so elusive that, after the end of the 19th century, it was believed to be extinct. But in 1948 Dr G.B. Orbell of Invercargill discovered otherwise, when he stumbled upon a takahe in a valley above Te Anau in Fiordland. The takahe is a plump, meaty bird, rather like a fat pukeko. (Dr Orbell confessed years later that, when he first saw one, he could imagine that it would make 'a good roast meal'.)

In the wild, the contemporary takahe has difficulty finding the food it needs, because imported deer eat the tussock on whose seeds it relies. And stoats eat the eggs and chicks. Those takahe that do survive are well looked after in reserves on a number of islands, as well as in the Murchison Mountains.

Q Takeaway

It would be impossible to pin down when or by whom eat-on-the-street food was invented. The peoples of China, Japan, India and most of Europe would look at you incredulously if you asked — they've done it for centuries, and they probably don't have a word for it.

The United States went into walkabout food in a big way, with patties of minced beef served between buns before the end of the 19th century (these have been called hamburgers since 1900, although there is absolutely no firm evidence as to *why*). Besides extending into cheeseburgers and vegeburgers and baconburgers, Americans developed hot dogs (named after a cartoon in the early 1900s showing a dachshund inside a bread roll). And the term fast food began to be used in the States from 1954 onwards. Two other expressions grew from this: takeout food and food to go.

These descriptions never really caught on in New Zealand. The term takeaway, which meant substantially the same thing and was coined in Britain in the late 1960s, was somehow preferable to the Kiwi tongue and has remained firmly entrenched, sometimes preceded by an adjective: Chinese takeaways, Indian takeaways, etc. Visitors and tourists unfamiliar with the term sometimes see the sign and assume it is a Maori word, to be pronounced 'tah-kee-ah-wey'.

 ## Taking a jack

It means having a look, or peering at. The expression is heard in New Zealand in two forms, the full 'taking a Jack Nohi', or the abbreviated 'taking a jack'.

The origin appears to be the Maori word for face, kanohi, and is obviously associated with looking. But, over time, pronunciation was corrupted into Jack Nohi and then shortened to just 'a jack'.

 ## Tall poppy

A tall poppy is a person of considerable success, a high-profile achiever. New Zealand shares suspicion of success with Australia, which is where this term originated in approximately 1900. The term grew in prominence in 1931 when politician J. Laing referred to a tax that would 'cut the heads off the tall poppies' (i.e. the wealthy). Since then the term has become used to include not just the wealthy but the big noters and those with their heads sticking above the parapets.

When used as a verb, the term has developed a curious negative version of itself: to tall poppy someone is to ensure that they are cut down to size and their head is no longer above the parapet.

 ## Tamarillo

Tamarillo is a totally invented word. The fruit itself is native to the Andes and to India, from where New Zealand's first seeds came in 1891. There are many different varieties: when New Zealanders first grew them, the fruit was yellow or purple. But from the 1920s onwards the red-skinned species achieved great popularity under the name tree tomato although, apart from its colour, the fruit had little resemblance to a tomato and certainly tasted quite different.

In 1967 the name tamarillo replaced the former name. It was contrived by starting with tomato, then replacing the suffix '-ato' with '-ill' (to indicate small). The resulting word tomatillo was altered again to include a Maori element: it became tamatillo, which was then softened to tamarillo.

 ## Tangata whenua

Maori for the people of the land, this expression is a way of distinguishing Maori people from all others. The expression carries the unspoken connotation that whoever it is applied to has been a person of the land of New Zealand *since antiquity*. Even non-Maori New Zealanders of the fourth of fifth generation within this country are not included within the term.

 ## Tangi

This Maori word carries images of weeping and sadness, an occasion for mourning, and so it is the usual word for identifying what Europeans would call a funeral.

But the Maori image of death goes further than a straightforward religious service, usually followed by an interment. Correctly called tangihanga, Maori funeral rites can occupy several days, with the bereaved's body lying surrounded by family, while groups of relatives and friends, some of whom have travelled long distances, are afforded formal welcome ceremonies as they arrive.

Q Taonga

Maori for a treasure, a taonga can be something practical — a precious stone, a person, an artifact, a picture, even something very large like a piece of land, all the natural food available in an area, the native trees and birds. It can also be something ephemeral, such as a tradition, a prayer, the words of a song, a reputation or a set of beliefs.

Q Tap

It's a simple enough word which, among several meanings, includes the valve by which a fluid flow can be controlled by releasing or closing an opening. Every New Zealand bathroom, kitchen and garden has one or more.

But it's another of those words that Americans don't use, and look puzzled if a New Zealander directs them towards one. What they want is a faucet.

Q Tapu

The word taboo arrived in English about 1770, having been first heard in Tonga by English-speaking people. The Maori language has no b, so the New Zealand version of the word (substantially the same meaning as the Tongan) is tapu.

Within New Zealand the two words, taboo and tapu, exist side by side. But their meanings vary slightly. In accordance with Polynesian usage, tapu indicates that something is forbidden because it is sacred or connected with a spiritual matter. The more common English version, taboo, somehow omits the connotation of being forbidden for spiritual reasons, and tends to mean just forbidden. Often the reason for the forbidding is moral rather than religious.

A New Zealander recognises that an area declared tapu by Maori elders must not be wandered around for reasons of spiritual protocol, whereas having loud conversations in a library is merely a taboo.

 ## Taranaki gate

A rough-and-ready (but efficient) construction of sticks and wire which serves as a gate, the Taranaki gate is often part of a fence — perhaps where a road or driveway goes through. A section of the fence is constructed separately, hinged on wire loops at one end, and secured by wire loops at the other end, so the gate can be opened and shut. Usually they are three or four vertical wooden battens held together by horizontal strands of wire, often barbed wire. The kind of gate was certainly more widespread than just the province of Taranaki and the term may have been in use for some decades before it appeared in print in 1937.

New Zealand farm fences and wire gates have a distinctive look. The animated movie *Footrot Flats* had some of its artwork done in Australia, and parts of it had to be sent back and redone, because the Australian animators' view of a farm fence simply didn't look right to the New Zealand producers.

 ## Taranaki salute

The lush and beautiful area of Taranaki is orientated towards the dairy industry and is also populated by people of eminent pragmatism and a notable ability at self-deprecation. This results in such local expressions as Taranaki salute — gumboots being stamped in order to shake off cow dung (which itself is known as Taranakai top dressing); rain and drizzle is referred to as Taranaki sunshine; the sound of cowbells is sometimes called Taranaki violins; and Taranaki drive is a method of felling one tree deliberately so it falls on another and eventually results in several trees falling.

Q Taranaki wool

In the 1870s, a Chinese merchant named Chew Chong was buying up scrap metal in New Zealand and exporting it to China. Travelling in Taranaki he noticed a fungus growing on rotting logs, very similar to a similar flattish mushroom that grew in China and was considered a great delicacy there.

Chew Chong set himself up in New Plymouth and organised the gathering and export of this fungus, which gained the name Taranaki wool. He exported huge amounts of the fungus before shifting his attention to New Zealand butter, which he managed to export to England; he opened his first dairy factory in 1885. He thus became a pioneer in New Zealand's dairy export industry.

Tartan

Tartan is the characteristic Scottish design of coloured lines and bands intersecting to form squares. New Zealanders (with a strong Scottish heritage) tend to use the word correctly: meaning the square design itself. Elsewhere the fabric and its design is sometimes referred to as plaid, which strictly means only the shawl draped over the shoulder in Scottish national dress.

Taumatawhakatangihangakoauauotamatea-pokaiwhenuakitanatahu

It is unwise ever to claim anything as the first, the biggest or the longest, for surely another will emerge that beats the claim. Therefore this place name should wisely be referred to as *one of the longest place names in the world* (a locality in Wales is said to equal it).

It commemorates an adventure of Tamatea-Pokai-Whenua, a long-ago Maori traveller. A 300-metre hill in Hawke's Bay carries the above name, which in English means 'The brow of the hill where Tamatea, the man with the big knees who slid, climbed and swallowed mountains, known as Traveller, played on his flute to his loved one'. In common usage, the hill is simply referred to as Taumata.

 ## Te Reo

Although the Maori word reo means voice or speech, it is usually used to mean language, and most specifically the Maori language. An adjective is sometimes added so that 'te reo Pakeha' would mean the English language. But used unadorned, te reo usually indicates the Maori language.

 ## Terminal lift

The formal name for a curious vocal habit, endlessly analysed by linguists as 'a characteristic speech rhythm of New Zealanders', in which the voice is suddenly raised to a slightly higher tone at the end of almost every sentence — the result being a faintly questioning air, even when the syntax doesn't suggest this. Also known as rising intonation, the speech pattern is clearly discernible and has been for many years, but there is no stable explanation for why this happens. Sometimes the terminal lift has been described as showing a lack of inner confidence — that every statement requires return assurance.

 ## Thermette

Designed to boil water, this narrow metal cylinder has a tubular chimney up through the middle, reaching from the base to an open top. Newspapers or twigs burned in the central cylinder boil the water very quickly.

The 'rapid boiler' was invented in New Zealand by John Hart in the late 1920s, and in 1936 a patent application was entered for the device itself and the trade name Thermette. It is an extremely successful invention, domestically for picnicking and camping, and also for the military. New Zealand troops supplied with these in North Africa during the Second World War referred to them jocularly as Benghazi burners or Benghazi boilers.

There you go

A common expression of acknowledgement, roughly equivalent to the French *voila* or Italian *ecco*. It can signify a variety of meanings: 'Here you are' (as in handing someone a drink); 'How surprising!'(when told something alarming); 'I'm listening to you but I don't agree with you'; 'Isn't that what you'd expect to happen!'

Thrashing

The various meanings of thrash all seem to follow a pattern: they concern using an object to give violent beatings to a person, to wheat, to water, or to lunge about in a random manner. But at least two other shades of meaning have developed in New Zealand.

First, there is the use of a qualifier, such as good. To give someone a good thrashing seems a contradiction in terms, since a beating can hardly ever be good (from the recipient's point of view), but the term is nevertheless widely used. In this context, 'good' is not meant to indicate morally worthy or pleasant, but instead a sense of being thorough.

Second, as well as actually beating someone in order to punish them, New Zealanders use the word thrashing to describe the treatment of some factor — mechanical, natural or philosophical — that has been overused, overworked or stretched to maximum capacity.

This thrashing of the non-human and non-responsive allows for no fighting back and can involve a vehicle such as a tractor or a car being given a thrashing — being used relentlessly or at high speed; a bush area that has had a thrashing because overhunting has thinned out the animals; or a discussion where some theory is

217

discussed exhaustively and maybe argumentatively — it has been given a thrashing or even thrashed out.

A thrashing can also refer to the heavy defeat of a sports team.

 Throw a wobbly

To throw a wobbly is to lose control, display bad temper and generally have a tantrum. The expression became common in New Zealand during the 1960s and may even have originated here. It appears to be just an economical verbal description of a person's behaviour while in the grip of brief passionate frustration. The existence of a similar and older expression, throw a fit, suggests that wobbly has simply been substituted to indicate that the person is wobbling with anger.

By the 1980s, to throw a wobbly had become an easily understood expression in many places besides New Zealand.

 Thuh

For many decades New Zealand followed the standard English custom of pronouncing 'the' as *thee* in front of a vowel, and *thuh* before a consonant. But late in the 20th century came the placing of one open vowel next to another, which required the introduction of a glottal stop — a brief stopping of breath in the windpipe in order to create a vocal gap between one sound and the next.

Speakers of German or Tongan do it all the time as a natural part of those particular languages, but the device was virtually unknown in received standard English until English-speakers inexplicably decided to introduce it. The custom is now fairly universal in New Zealand, is commonly heard in Parliament and even a National Radio reporter will say: '*Thuh* office of *thuh* Environment provided *thuh* Air Force to bring *thuh* aid which *thuh* eastern part of *thuh* island needed'.

(There are also signs that New Zealanders may abandon the custom of *a* before a consonant and *an* before a vowel. A radio news report commented on a VIP's 'support for a Upper House in Parliament' while advertisers often promise 'a excellent bargain'. This new practice requires the same glottal stop, so that a banana is now sometimes joined by a apple and a orange.)

 **Tiger**

Apart from it obviously meaning a wonderful striped animal, during the 19th century tiger developed a meaning in New Zealand and Australia to describe someone who is enthusiastic and eager, usually for work, or for high standards.

It can confuse visitors when used in the expression, a tiger for punishment, which doesn't actually mean that someone wants to be punished but that he or she is ready and willing to take on complex and tiring projects and does not look for an easy path.

Q Tiki

An artifact — often a piece of jewellery, especially a pendant — showing a stylised human figure unique to Maori art. The figure is almost foetal in form, although it evokes a sense of being powerful rather than vulnerable. Within Maori legend, tiki is the name for the creator of humankind, so one connotation of a tiki is that it represents the first man, and therefore one's ancestors. Correctly, the figure's full name is heitiki but the shorter version, tiki, is considered acceptable in informal circumstances.

Q Tiki tour

The word tiki is attractive and features in the titles of trade organisations wishing to establish instantly that their goods or services are uniquely New Zealand. But besides naming a perfectly respectable package-travel organisation, the expression tiki tour has taken on a common side meaning, namely to take a long, unnecessarily complicated route. It is said of taxi drivers who either don't know their territory or who deliberately spin out the kilometres of their drive. It can describe a person in an unfamiliar city seeking a post office and becoming waylaid or confused while doing so. Instead of going directly from one place to another, they are (usually unwillingly) doing a tiki tour.

 Tin

It's a simple enough word, but it sometimes confuses visitors. Because such foods as baked beans and preserved fruits are sold in a tin can, New Zealanders refer to this as a tin, and to the goods therein as tinned. The supermarkets agree: their signs point us towards tinned fruit. The usage extends to beer when it's sold in a can — it is sometimes referred to as a tinnie (or occasionally as a tube).

Other cultures, however, always refer to such fruit, vegetables, beer etc. as canned and sold in a can.

The advent of lightweight plastic-type aluminium has not affected the New Zealand terminology at all — they are still called tins.

(A Chinese person who came to live in New Zealand had the genuine name Tinn Kan and was gently advised by authorities to adopt a different nomenclature.)

 Tinny

Possibly extending an old slang term for money, tin, in modern times the adjective means lucky, likely to succeed, blessed with the ability to overcome apparent difficulties. Sometimes extended to saying someone lucky has a tin bum.

(Note the difference when spelt tinnie, which refers to a can of beer.)

Q Tip

It is an area put aside where rubbish is placed, or tipped. Americans might call it a garbage dump. Some visitors are very confused, in places of natural beauty, such as a beach, to find signs that read: 'No tipping, by order of city council': they think this means they're not allowed to give money to restaurant waiters. They might expect the sign to say, 'No trash or garbage dumping'.

Q Toey

Toey is short-tempered, irascible, on edge — like a horse toeing the ground with its hooves. An equivalent term in the United States is antsy, meaning restive because of ants in the pants.

Q Togs

At the start of summer, every good Kiwi decides whether it's time for new swimming togs. Why togs? Surprisingly enough, the word is great-grandson of the Latin word *toga*, which meant clothes in general, not just the sweeping draperies of the senators.

The Latin original surfaces at least twice in contemporary English — as a shorthand for a swimming costume, and in an expression pertaining to particularly special clothes, as in being all togged up.

So when you put the word swimming in front of the word togs you get clothes for swimming, even if Speedos don't look anything like your actual historic toga.

Q Too right

A frequent statement of affirmation, it simply means, indeed, yes, or, I am in full agreement.

Q Top dressing

This is often used as an abbreviation for aerial top dressing. Terrestrial top dressing — spreading fertiliser of some kind onto soil at ground level — has been practised for centuries. New Zealand started the practice of distributing fertiliser over a rural area by flying across in a fairly low plane equipped with hoppers which feed the fertiliser out by release mechanisms. This method of aerial fertilising was first suggested in New Zealand in 1926 but didn't actually happen until 1936 (on the first occasion the plane distributed pasture seed). Steady growth of faith in the effectiveness of the operation eventually made aerial top dressing a normal part of New Zealand agricultural activity. In some countries it is called crop dusting.

Q Trailers

To an American a trailer is what New Zealanders call a caravan. But in common New Zealand usage the trailer is the short piece of film showing highlights from a movie which is about to be released, or shown at that venue. Trailer has actually replaced the earlier term, the shorts, by which New Zealanders meant all the various bits of film shown before the intermission, when movie showings customarily had intermissions.

Journalist and film reviewer Michael Lamb once queried why the preview highlights are referred to as trailers when they are shown *before* the film is released. It is reminiscent of famous New Zealand author Janet Frame reporting her childhood confusion about a process of hairdressing called permanent waves, which in the event turn out not to be permanent at all.

Perhaps aware of the illogicality, the movie industry doesn't use the word trailer and tends to refer to these mini-previews of movies as teasers or promos.

Treaty of Waitangi

The nation of New Zealand has no actual written constitution. The Treaty of Waitangi, which is known as New Zealand's founding document, is an agreement, signed by Maori chiefs over a period of six months during 1840. (Signing started on 6 February in Waitangi, Bay of Islands, and finished on 3 September.) It has been subject to deep controversy ever since, starting with its very name, since the word treaty is commonly held to mean a contract between two or more nation states — and this one isn't.

Its original form has never become law and interpretations of concepts such as partnership have been grafted onto the original wording (there is no mention of partnership in the original).

Two other surprising omissions in the original are:

(1) There is no mention of the British nation, the British government or the Crown. The agreement is only with Queen Victoria, who is referred to 11 times.

(2) No continuance of agreement is established, there being no mention of the treaty remaining in place with Victoria's heirs and successors (she was 20 at the time and was married in the month that the treaty signing began).

A national holiday is held each year on 6 February, the day on which the first signatures went onto the document. But since the agreement is solely with Victoria, whose successors were not acknowledged, one school of thought believes that the treaty came to a legal end in 1901, when Victoria died.

Q **The trots**

These are either Montezuma's revenge (diarrhoea) or a race meeting with trotting or pacing races — harness racing — in which sulkies, light two-wheeled vehicles, are driven by one person and pulled by one horse.

Q Tuatara

Tuatara don't get a telegram on their 100th birthday, though they might possibly qualify for more than one because each tuatara (a lizard-like reptile) is thought to live for 200 years or more. The first one seen by a European, John Gray in 1831, might well still be alive. In ancestry, the tuatara is immeasurably old — more than 200 million years — and it is believed to have remained unchanged for all that time. The mysterious depression in its forehead, sometimes called a vestige of a third eye, actually has nerve-end collections, probably for heat-sensing. Slow moving, the tuatara has not coped well with imported predators, and can only live safely on islands that have no weasels, ferrets, cats or rats. They eat wetas, crickets, beetles and worms, other lizards and occasional small birds. It must be a healthy diet, as tuatara grow to be very old citizens indeed.

Q Turkeys

Unlike Santa Claus, who came from Turkey, turkeys originate from South America, and the name was a terrible mistake. When the bird was introduced to England it was confused with the guinea fowl (itself something of a novelty at the time), which originated in Muslim West Africa. Since Turkey is also a mainly Muslim country, casual association of the Muslim religion with the two (quite different) birds eventually resulted in the newer one somehow acquiring the name turkey, quite erroneously. (The particular recognisable blue-black species was mostly found in Mexico.)

As part of Christmas, turkeys are something of a latecomer. They didn't reach England until 1535 and it was another couple of hundred years before they became popular Christmas fare, because by then the number of wild boars (the original traditional Christmas meat) was seriously depleted.

In New Zealand, the use of turkeys as Christmas fare has always been something of a worry since, unlike the northern hemisphere, turkeys are not in their prime in December. For many years New Zealand farmers with access to large wholesale freezers killed their turkeys in winter (any month with no r in it) when the birds had eaten their fill and fattened up, then retrieved them from the freezer in mid-December. More recently, commercial organisations have streamlined much the same process and made frozen turkeys generally available during December.

In New Zealand's contemporary decades, a vigorous strain of albino turkeys has made noticeable inroads into the glossy black colour of traditional turkeys (known as bronze-wing) which are now often a glossy salt-and-pepper mottled. Fortunately they taste the same.

U

Up the booai

It's spelt various ways, but the meaning is always clear — way, way out, a long way from cities, off centre, out of the mainstream. The origin is pure Kiwi and somewhat Auckland-based.

During the 19th century immigrants arrived in Auckland from the region of Czechoslovakia then called Bohemia. For reasons of language and fellowship they nearly all gravitated to a settlement slightly north of Auckland called Puhoi.

The average city-dweller considered Puhoi to be absolutely too far away to be taken seriously, and the very word took on a shade of meaning somewhat like the back of beyond. And the 'foreign' locals who lived there had a little trouble pronouncing Puhoi accurately. In time, Puhoi became 'booai', meaning truly isolated.

The up came a little bit later, along with such nonsensical additions as 'growing rhubarb' or 'shooting pukekos with a broom handle'.

Nowadays a smooth tarsealed road leads effortlessly to the charming rural village of Puhoi (still with many traces of its Bohemian settlers), but the expression remains.

Unit

(1) Within a motel complex, a unit is the accommodation space available for one booking. The term is commonly used in this way throughout New Zealand but is often completely unknown to visitors.

(2) A home unit is a permanent dwelling, usually on one level, built as a detached or semi-detached and independent part of a

larger building or interrelated cluster of buildings.

(3) An electric train used on some suburban routes.

 ## Ute

An abbreviation for a small (but feisty) utility vehicle, known elsewhere as a pick-up truck. The word 'utility' is often applied to vehicles in other places, but tends not to have the same down-home connotation of New Zealanders in their go-anywhere-carry-anything utes.

 ## Utu

The casual translation of this Maori word is revenge, but that does not give the full picture. To engage in and succeed in an act of utu means that satisfaction has been achieved — possibly over a wrong righted, or a return, a reward, even a compensation.

The carrying out of utu may not always be harsh or violent — though at times in history it has been, if the original act being righted or compensated for was itself harsh and violent. In those circumstances, and only those, utu could be translated as revenge.

Van

If there was a prize for the most misunderstood word in a national anthem, New Zealand would have to win, with its deathless phrase 'Guide us in the nations' van (preaching love and truth to man).' Generations of schoolchildren have been convinced it's probably something to do with delivering pizza.

But this van isn't the four-wheeled kind. It is short for vanguard. Unfortunately, even that word has become rather obsolete. If you told the school choir that they were asking God to guide us in the vanguard they probably wouldn't be much wiser.

Vanguard means the leading position in any movement, the people who occupy such a position, the division that leads an army. Vanguard itself is actually short for avant garde.

So 'guide us in the nations' van' is actually asking that New Zealand, as a nation, be helped to keep up front.

(See also **National Anthem**)

Q Vegemite

Expatriate New Zealanders write letters begging their families and friends to send a jar of it. New Zealanders going on a trip overseas take it with them. It is part of our culinary landscape — and often puzzling to outsiders. A London journalist nibbled some, then wrote of its flavour: 'Can you imagine eating the smell of unwashed socks?' An American magazine, by contrast, advised readers to 'ignore the flavour and just remember that because of its high vitamin B content, this mixture is likely to be an effective aphrodisiac'.

Vegemite was actually invented by an industrial chemist in Melbourne, who was working on ways of improving brewer's yeast. At one stage he put baker's yeast into the mixture and wondered if the result might be edible. Everyone has been cagey ever since about exactly what ingredients were added in the experiment, but it seems to revolve around the original yeast, plus celery and onions.

The manufacturers were considering naming the product Parwill but decided to hold a competition among the public in case a better name came up. Because the spread had no animal products, a bright spark thought up the name Vegemite and won the competition.

Vegemite has been manufactured since 1925 (in Australia) and began New Zealand production in 1958. In their 1989 book, *New Zealand! New Zealand! In Praise of Kiwiana*, Richard Wolfe and Stephen Barnett revealed that, by then, New Zealanders were buying 2.2 million jars of it each year. Nobody has ever had the courage to estimate how many school lunches that would be.

Vet

This is not a new word in New Zealand, but it now has two meanings. There was a time when vet was short for veterinarian, a person who looked after the medical needs of animals. There were city vets who were good with pedigree cats and poodles, country vets who could cope with the problems of cows and sheep, and racing club vets who specialised in horses. In those days, people who had fought in wars were called ex-servicemen or returned servicemen.

But in the United States people who had survived wars were called veterans, abbreviated to vets. In the kind of linguistic osmosis to which New Zealanders have been prone for many years, when they heard American movies and news reports referring to vets meaning ex-military people, they adopted the usage themselves.

Nowadays in New Zealand when somebody says the word vet it is wise to ask, 'Which kind?'

Q Wag

Of course it means wave from side to side, as in a dog's tail, and connected with that is the common New Zealand usage — to side-slip, to bypass, to take time off unofficially, play truant (especially from school or employment). Americans call it playing hookey.

New Zealand also retains the ancient British wag, meaning a pleasant and amusing rascal (from the Old English *waghalter* — a person who shakes the halter).

Q Waiata

Literally translated into English, the Maori word waiata means a shape that flows, thus a song. The term covers all forms of song — from the pre-European waiata, which resembles Gregorian chant in its unaccompanied complexity, to contemporary compositions with soloists, choir and complex instrumental backings.

Q Waka

In literal terms the Maori word waka means container, and can apply to several kinds of small box or receptacle. It is most usually heard to describe a large Maori canoe and can also mean the crew of that canoe, or the descendants of early immigrants who arrived in one of the great canoes of Maori mythology.

(The general meanings of receptacle and canoe can be flexible.

Out shopping in the city one day, a Maori woman met a friend and was heard to say, 'Where did you park your waka?')

 Washing

In New Zealand the verb 'to wash' is known in its usual meaning — to clean something with water. But as 'the washing' it becomes slightly different. This is shorthand for garments that must be cleaned and dried, often on a regular weekly basis. Hanging out the washing means pegging the wet, cleaned clothes on a line to dry.

In other countries this is often called the laundry, as is the place in which the operation is carried out. New Zealanders used to do the washing in a separate outside room called the wash house, but the invention of compact electric washing machines meant that the wash house could come inside the house. Now this room is usually called the laundry.

 Whaddarya?

This rather insulting rhetorical question is said derisively to a person (usually male) when you wish to call into doubt his courage, his quality as a person and suggest that perhaps he does not qualify as a real bloke. The term featured prominently in Greg McGee's hit play *Foreskin's Lament* in 1980 and has been in common use ever since.

Q Weta

A well-known local insect, the weta is related to grasshoppers, locusts and crickets, but is much more fearsome in appearance than any of those. Weta are long and narrow with no wings, prominent angular legs (with nasty spines on them), shiny brown armour all over and frightening primeval faces.

A 45-millimetre weta is fairly normal, but the giant North Island species can reach 65 millimetres in length and is among the largest insects in the world.

Other kinds of weta can be found in South Africa, Chile, Australia and parts of the United States. New Zealand has nearly 100 different kinds of indigenous weta. Tree and cave weta are the most common, being found in gardens, hedges, orchards and among old bits of wood. They are usually harmless, but finding one unexpectedly can cause a fright because of their *Jurassic Park*-like appearance.

 ## Whanau

The Maori word whanau is best translated as immediate family. A person's grandparents, parents, the other children of those parents (i.e. the person's own sisters and brothers) and the person's own children — that is whanau.

 ## Whinge

It is a British dialect version of the Old English *hwinsian* — to fret and complain — which developed into whinge.

Although whinge went out of use almost entirely in Britain, it had travelled to New Zealand and Australia during the 19th century, and is still in general currency here (especially in the associated term whingeing Pom, meaning a constantly dissatisfied Englishman). In the mid-20th century the word started to be used in Britain again and people vaguely thought of it as being antipodean, not realising that it had been British in the first place.

 ## Whitebait

In New Zealand the term whitebait is used to describe the juveniles of the inanga, a fish commonly found in lowland rivers and streams.

Soon after hatching in estuaries, the very young fish head out to sea for a period and then attempt to return to fresh water.

The young whitebait is a very thin, almost-transparent fish the thickness of a medium knitting needle and with prominent eyes. A good many of them are needed to make any sort of a meal. Usually handfuls are fried in a binding batter.

The name whitebait was being used to describe them as early as 1840, and has been used consistently ever since. This causes mild confusion for British people, since for them whitebait is an entirely different fish, the young of the sprat, shad and herring.

 ## White goods, whiteware

These are major household electrical appliances. At some time in the development of electricity, all major electrical goods were enamelled white, and many still are. But even when finished in fashionable pastels, wood tones or even shiny steel, they are still frequently referred to as whiteware.

 ## Wopcacker

Combining elements of two other words, whopper and cracker-jack, wopcacker appears to have surfaced in Australia in the 1920s and migrated to New Zealand some 20 years later. It means that something is huge, impressive, outstanding or surprising.

Over the decades there have been various spellings — whop-cacker, woopcacker, even woopknacker — but since the word isn't a formal part of the language and the pronunciation is only marginally affected, none of these variations matter.

For a time in the 1950s, a somewhat outlandish drink consisted of pure gin placed in a glass and, with one hand firmly over the top, shaken vigorously. It made a surprising amount of supremely alcoholic froth which had to be drunk quickly if the effect was to be enjoyed. It was named a gin wopcacker.

Q Wop-wops

Early British settlers to Australian were amused by the number of Aboriginal place names with repeated syllables. The Britishers made up the word woop-woops as a satirical mock-native word, making fun of some of the existing native place names.

New Zealanders very soon adopted the word, using it to mean a place so distant that it has no real name, but in this country it is generally pronounced with shorter vowels as wop-wops.

Q Written off

This quasi-legal term, originating in Britain, refers to the cancelling of a bad debt or an obsolete asset — sometimes an asset being depreciated by regular charges against it — or to cause or acknowledge the complete loss of.

It was this last meaning that was taken up by the Royal Flying Corps in 1914: when an aircraft was completely wrecked it could be written off the inventory as of no further use. The usage extended to other vehicles — originally service vehicles smashed to a level where repairing them would not have been economic.

Another variation arose when people who were ineffective or useless began to be referred to as a write-off. Later in the 20th century, both variations of the term gradually extended to civilian life.

Within New Zealand the term has become very common, particularly in referring to smashed cars, whether uninsured (and uneconomic for the owner to repair) or insured (and equally uneconomic for the insurance company to repair).

Y

Q Yakking

In the late 1930s Americans were using the word yocking to indicate useless talk. The term went through various versions — including yucking — until by 1958 it seemed to settle down into yakking, or yackety yak: idle chatter, empty babble. It is possible that the word has some ancestor in Yiddish, but it is generally regarded as being echoic in origin — meaning that the word imitates what it is describing.

New Zealanders caught onto the word very quickly and it is commonly used.

Another frequently heard parallel term is the much older (1918) blah-di-blah-di-blah, a possible corruption of the German *blech* (nonsense), plus the echoic influence.

During the 1990s a popular television show engendered a new version of the same idea: yadda-yadda-yadda.

Q Ya'reckon?

Based on its meaning of calculate, the word reckon has taken on several shades of meaning in New Zealand, often as a statement of confident personal opinion rather than reasoned belief.

New Zealanders customarily use the word in a way that is both negative and positive. 'I reckon' is often a shorthand way of saying 'I agree with you' or 'In my opinion this is a good thing' or 'Yes, this is worthwhile'.

Also quite common is the question form, ya'reckon?, which still retains a shade of the calculate meaning, because it is really asking whether this is your considered opinion. Or even — 'I cannot agree with what you believe and am reluctant to listen to any more of it because I don't intend to change my mind.' New Zealanders realised decades ago that it was quicker to say ya'reckon?

 ## Yonks

The term, which means an indefinitely long time, did not originate in New Zealand but has been taken warmly to the nation's heart and is widely used. First noticed in the British Army in the 1950s, yonks is thought to be either a cryptic combination wrought from *y*ears, *mo*nths and wee*ks*, or a sloppy contraction of donkeys' years, meaning a long time (derived from donkey's ears, because they are long).

 ## Youse

One idiosyncrasy of the English language is that it has no specific word for the second-person-plural (like the French *vous* or German *Sie*). In English, saying 'you' can mean you're addressing just one other person, or a crowd of thousands.

But some people, feeling the lack of such a word, gradually developed a possible candidate: youse, meaning plural people I'm addressing. The word is categorised as non-standard, meaning that although its existence is reluctantly acknowledged, it is not a recognised word in the formal language. (In some British and American dialects it appears as yez.)

Many New Zealanders have cheerfully ignored the official ruling that the word is not part of the language. It was first printed in New Zealand in 1908 (as yewse) and has remained in frowned-upon use ever since, mainly for the plural 'you', but sometimes also for the singular.

Q Yummy

Derived from yum-yum and usually regarded as a child-like way of saying that a food is favourable and tasty, yummy has moved into moderate acceptability for adult usage in New Zealand and since the 1990s has been heard in conversational context and from cooks on television.

Q Zambuck

A popular abbreviation for the good people from the St John Ambulance organisation, who for many decades have been a familiar sight at sports matches and public events, standing by in case paramedical attention is needed.

The word zambuck could possibly have been achieved by rapidly saying St John Ambulance plus buck. But after 1900 a popular antiseptic ointment called Zambuck was being used in New Zealand (imported from the British-based Bile Bean Manufacturing Company!) and first-aid assistants commonly used it for many emergency purposes; it was also customarily rubbed into painful patches caused during vigorous sports. The name of the ointment became transferred to the people who administered it — the zambucks. The nickname stayed on even after the practice of using the ointment faded.

Q Zed

The last letter of the alphabet in New Zealand is pronounced zed, not zee. The letter we know as zed was the seventh letter of the Greek and Hebrew alphabets and became the 26th letter of the Roman alphabet, though they didn't use it much. Its use in English has always been fairly sparse, in fact it was sometimes considered not even needed — in Shakespeare's *King Lear* (Act 2, scene ii) you'll find the line 'Thou whoreson zed, thou unnecessary letter'. There have been several changes: many centuries ago in English, z was known as zed-bar and later became zad.

This had settled into zed by the time early British pilgrims started settling in America. There is no clear reason why Americans changed zed to zee but it is believed that, over time, they made an adjustment by analogy so that the pronunciation of the last letter of the alphabet fitted with the pronunciation of other letters, like b, c, d, g, p, t, v. This applied especially in that little rhyme children are taught, to the tune of 'Twinkle twinkle little star': A-B-C-D-E-F-G . . . etc. (This theory, which is only scholastic speculation, is hard to back up in that if the Americans had been consistent in this, then w would be pronounced 'wee'.)

New Zealand music entrepreneur Ray Columbus, when establishing an office in the United States some years ago, prudently named it EnZed, in order to ensure Americans would have to say zed, which he preferred. Later in 2001 when a young band put themselves in his care, Columbus decided they were worth an international career, and named them Zed, because the word had an intriguing exotic quality for the American market. And he was right.

It is sometimes said that when New Zealanders are travelling overseas they have a considerable facility for spotting a capital z on a newspaper page. Their eyes will go to it straightaway, hoping, of course, that the z presages a news item about home. Disappointingly, it usually doesn't. New Zealand author Debra Daley used this idea in her novel *The Strange Letter Z*.

 ## Zespri

This word came into being in 1997 when the New Zealand Kiwifruit Marketing Board decided that all kiwifruit were to be branded under that name. An international consulting firm was asked to provide a selection of names that conveyed the crisp flavour sensation of eating a kiwifruit. Rigorous tests were carried out on a group of possible names to ensure that they didn't inadvertently mean something unfortunate in a foreign language, that they had no underground offensive connotations or transgressed any cultural sensitivities.

Finally Zespri was chosen because of its 'energetic sound' and launched worldwide, with a very slight change in spelling for Chinese languages (in which Zespri caused a small difficulty in pronunciation).

At a similar time — late 1990s — the fruit market saw its first new gold-fleshed kiwifruit which, in accordance with the new marketing policy, was sold as Zespri Gold. This confused some people, who thought that Zespri meant only the golden kiwifruit: in fact it applies to them all, gold or green.

Bibliography and Sources

Barnett, Stephen and Richard Wolfe, *New Zealand! New Zealand! In Praise of Kiwiana*, Hodder & Stoughton, 1989.

Barnett, Stephen and Richard Wolfe, *Kiwiana! The Sequel*, Penguin, 2001.

Brewer's Dictionary of Modern Phrase and Fable, ed. Adrian Room, Cassell, 2000.

Brewer's Dictionary of Phrase and Fable, 15th edition, ed. Adrian Room, Cassell, 1996.

Brewer's Dictionary of Twentieth-Century Phrase and Fable, Cassell, 1991.

Chapman, Robert L. (ed.), *The Dictionary of American Slang*, Harper Perennial, 1998.

McGill, David, *A Dictionary of Kiwi Slang*, Mills Publications, 1988.

McGill, David, *The Complete Kiwi Slang Dictionary*, Reed Publishing (NZ) Ltd, 1998.

Orange, Claudia (ed.), *The Dictionary of New Zealand Biography, Volumes I – V*, Auckland University Press, 2000.

Orsman, H.W. (ed.), *The Dictionary of New Zealand English*, Oxford University Press, 1997.

Partridge, Eric, *A Concise History of Slang and Unconventional English*, ed. Paul Beale, Routledge, 1992.

Partridge, Eric, *A Dictionary of Catch Phrases*, Routledge and Kegan Paul, 1977.

Partridge, Eric, *Origins: A Short Etymological Dictionary of Modern English*, Book Club Associates, 1959.

Smith, Carl V., *From N to Z*, Hicks Smith & Wright, Wellington, 1947.

The New Shorter Oxford Dictionary of English, Clarendon Press, 1993.

The Reed Dictionary of New Zealand Place Names, A.W. Reed, 2002 edition.

CURIOUS QUESTIONS

What are bugger grips?
Why are potatoes called spuds?
What is the origin of the term redneck?
Was Sweet Fanny Adams ever a real person?

These and other curious questions have been sent to Max Cryer
for over three years, and every Saturday morning he has answered
them on National Radio with his customary wit and authority.
Now Max has compiled a book of questions (and answers!) from
the first three years of his popular 'Curious Questions' slot. The
questions focus on the quirks of the English language, the origins
of unusual words and popular expressions, and the particular way
in which New Zealanders use the language. Arranged
alphabetically by key word, this book is a goldmine of information,
to be dipped into for reference or pleasure.

HarperCollins*Publishers*